Published by Gene Carman

genecarman@att.net

ISBN: 9781481053211

Printed in the United States of America

November 2012

This book is dedicated to all the men with whom I served. The telling of this story evokes memories of that era and are not completely told in this narrative, simply because some are vague and without backup to authenticate them. Others just don't need to be included— this isn't meant to be a "tell-all" book. Suffice it to say that with all the bad events related herein, there were offsetting good times, too. The events are truly told and documented. The crew performed as a caring, cohesive group and I am honored to have served with them. They are:

> LT Joe Maywald, pilot
> F/O Ed Weaver, co-pilot
> SGT Andy Citara, engineer/gunner
> SGT Richard Makoviac, radio operator/waist gunner
> SGT John Sequenz, tail gunner

Acknowledgements:

Cover photo courtesy of Greatest Generation Aircraft, www.gga1.org

My profound appreciation to Jeff Miller and the wonderful Special Addendum he provided for this book. In it he tells us all about how HonorAir began, how it evolved, and where it is today. We WWII veterans owe Jeff and his merry band a world of thanks for all they've done for us. Jeff had a ton of help getting HonorAir up and running and, while he won't accept any personal praise for what that project has accomplished, he's definitely the straw that stirred the drink. Thank you, Jeff, from all of us.

Gene Carman, September 21, 1943

TABLE OF CONTENTS

Page

INTRODUCTION
By Ed Nielsen

In March, 2012, several writer friends and I gathered for lunch. Also in attendance was Gene Carman, a gentleman I'd never met before. Although not a writer, Gene was a good friend of several others in our group. As you might expect, the conversation eventually got around to writing and the books we'd published. Okay, to be honest, the conversation started on that subject and stayed there. Gene listened attentively but didn't have much to add.

The other writers touted their books and I touted mine. In case you're not familiar, mine are *Warriors*, nine first-person accounts from the Vietnam War; and *Classical Classics*, 126 CD reviews and 10 essays on various aspects of classical music.

At the end of our lunch session, we all exchanged business cards, including Gene. As we turned to leave, Gene said to me, "I may be in touch. Would that be okay?"

I told him that'd be just fine.

"I served in WWII," he explained. "I got shot down over France. My friends and family have been after me to write about my war experiences, but writing a book is just not in me. I'm hoping you'd be willing to help."

Boy was he talking to the right guy. I had just finished publishing a book and suffered from withdrawal—I feel best when I'm in the middle of a writing project.

To make a long story short, Gene called me a week or so later and we arranged an interview. I brought a tape recorder and we had our first conversation of many. I immediately noticed how modest he was, very matter-of-fact, and not above mentioning his shortcomings.

At the time we started doing interviews for this book, Gene was not quite 94 years old. I couldn't help but notice how clear his recollections were, how sharp his memory for detail. I kept saying to myself, *Maybe I can be that lucid when I get to be his age.* I quickly abandoned that hope, realizing there was no way I could improve that much in the intervening years.

Coincidentally, Gene flew his very first combat mission on the day I was born!

At several points during our interview sessions, Gene had to pause, usually when discussing the demise of one of his crewmates or a similar event. At one such point, he just couldn't continue, overcome with emotion. He commented, "You'll have to excuse me for a minute. Gee, I thought I was over all that stuff."

After 70 years, he still gets dewy-eyed and has trouble speaking when recalling certain events. That tells all of us quite a bit about the depth of the relationships he created with his crewmates.

Gene asked me to tell you this: "English teachers taught me to avoid using 'they' in my writing, to avoid things like 'They told us to fly to Verona.' Teachers don't like that because readers may not know who *they* are. If I happen to use the word 'they' in this book, I'm talking about school directors, superior officers, and the like. So please excuse me if I occasionally forget what those English teachers taught me."

The first time they are used, we've explained most terms that may not be familiar to everyone. They are also defined in the Glossary. We have not defined such things as B-26 bomber or .45 automatic. To avoid slowing you down as you read, you may want to scan the Glossary to familiarize yourself with some of these terms.

Tom Brokaw nailed it when he called WWII veterans "The Greatest Generation." I'm so happy and proud that one of them chose me to help him tell his story. If you enjoy reading it just half as much as I've enjoyed writing it, you'll be very pleased indeed.

PROLOGUE

I remember from high school having to memorize the song, *The Bridge at Avignon*. Now my crew and I were on our way there—to bomb the place! On bombing runs, our normal objective was to take out railway bridges or marshalling yards. The bridge was there but on this mission we were after the marshalling yards. The marshalling yards were a series of train tracks where railcars could be pulled in, reconfigured into different trains, and routed out as necessary. We were sent to destroy the marshalling yards in order to disrupt enemy freight distribution.

The day was just beautiful, bright, sunshiny, clear, no clouds, just a very nice day. The intelligence we received during our pre-flight briefing led us to believe that there wouldn't be much flak (anti-aircraft fire) over Avignon, and that made us hopeful.

We took off anticipating we'd be able to get in and out easily, and that everything was going to be fine. Our planes were wheels-up at around nine in the morning. The crew I was on that day wasn't the same crew I had gone with to Corsica. I had volunteered to fly with another crew to replace its ill bombardier and to rack up more points toward leaving the war zone.

There were three echelons of aircraft in our flight, each composed of three B-25 bombers. After the first echelon, the planes in the succeeding echelons were spread out a bit. The strategy of this was that, by spreading out, we were almost guaranteed to hit our target. On a bomb run, each plane in the formation focused on the lead plane, the middle plane in the first echelon. When that plane dropped its load, all others also dropped theirs. Each bombardier had his bombsight operative and ready to take over should anything prevent the lead plane from leading as expected. In all of my missions that never happened.

The lead plane zeroed in on the main target. In the event of a "near miss" by the lead plane the trailing echelons would probably hit the target. If the lead echelon's bombs were on target, the trailing echelons would inflict peripheral damage and that was fine, too. When we bombed a marshalling yard, for example, this technique guaranteed maximum damage. We'd blow the whole rail yard apart, making it completely unusable.

Also, succeeding echelons flew at slightly different altitudes so they wouldn't fly into the foil released from the planes ahead of them. We carried in each of our planes a thing called a "window," long strips of metallic foil. As we approached the target, we'd drop the window to confuse the enemy radar on the ground. Their radar would focus on the window, which would be fluttering all over the sky. The objective was to give the enemy gunners trouble getting us in their sights.

At one time, only the lead ship would drop the window. In those days, succeeding planes would fly at the same altitude and run right into the window. That could cause engine damage. Plus, enemy guns below would be focusing on the window and that's exactly where the trailing planes were located. Flyers quickly saw the error of their ways and trailing planes began flying higher than the lead planes and weren't as susceptible to ground fire. That also ensured that trailing planes would be above the foil dropped from planes ahead.

We got to Avignon and could see the target very distinctly, no problem. We got to the drop point and that day my plane was in the lead echelon, to the right of the lead plane. We were to drop our bombs when he dropped his. We had everything set in our own bombsights and were ready to go. When he opened his bomb bay doors, we opened ours. When he dropped his bombs, we dropped, too, regardless of what our bombsights showed. The lead bombardier usually hit the main target and the rest of us inflicted additional damage in the general vicinity.

As we approached Avignon, we weren't expecting much flak. But our intelligence was a bit behind the power curve because the Germans had moved in a bunch of stuff that we didn't know about. Thus, the flak was very intense.

If there had to be flak, I always liked to see it off in the distance or far to the side. That way I knew where it was. But when we were approaching a target and the sky ahead of us was full of flak, I'd think, *God bless our pilots!* They had to look at that stuff and fly right into it—that took guts. Me, I could just concentrate on my bombsight, get focused on that, and almost forget about the flak.

A B-25 Bomber (not mine)

On a bombing run, we'd fly to what we called the IP, or Initial Point, and once there we opened the bomb bay doors and fine tuned our bomb sights on the target, getting the cross hairs in the sight to hold steady. We had 30 seconds from the IP to the drop point when our bombs would be released. The enemy gunners on the ground below also had the same 30 seconds to get us in their sights.

Sometimes when we heard flak it sounded like popcorn being popped. That was okay because that meant it was off in the distance and not an immediate danger. But we knew they were shooting at us and that's always a problem. The louder the sound, the closer the flak was to us.

When we dropped our bombs that day, I watched through the Plexiglas nose of the plane to see where our bombs were going to hit. About that same instant I heard a very loud BANG and felt the shudder. We'd been hit. We soon found out that the right rudder was gone, the B-25 being a twin-tail aircraft. Also, the right engine had been shot up and wasn't functioning at all, and the left engine was wind-milling, barely working. We knew we were going down.

My immediate instinct was to plot a course to Switzerland, but I looked at my map and saw there was no way we could make it over the Alps with our plane damaged so badly.

I had a steel ring on my ring finger that my brother had made for me. A piece of flak had hit that ring and glanced off into my little finger where it lodged. I didn't realize it at the time, but I also had several tiny pieces of Plexiglas in my nose and a slash on my left leg.

As soon as we were hit, I got on the intercom to see if everyone else was okay. No one else on the plane had been hit. That was miraculous, really something when you consider how shot to pieces the plane was.

Joe Maywald, our pilot, came on the intercom and said he knew we were going down. "Do you guys want to jump?" he asked, giving us the option.

I answered by asking, "Joe, can you handle this?"

He replied, "All the hydraulic systems are out and the manual system is tough to handle. But I honestly think I can bring it down."

He and the co-pilot, Ed Weaver, were very good pilots and we had confidence in them. If they said they could handle the damaged plane, we believed them.

I came back on-line and said I was staying, and the rest of the crew did the same. Andy Citara was our engineer/gunner, Richard Makoviac the waist-gunner/radioman, and John Sequenz the tail-gunner.

A B-25 with no power glides like a rock and we barely had any power at all, so we couldn't stay airborne for long. We were over southern France in occupied territory. Joe had picked a field that he thought would be a good place to land, but Ed spotted another one that he thought would be even better, offering a little more room. They managed to get the plane turned for an approach to that field.

We had made our approach in our crippled plane and weren't going to change it—we couldn't—when we noticed a rock wall running across the near end of the field. If you've been to Europe, you know that rock walls are very common there. The farmers had picked up the rocks in their fields and used them to make walls or fences to divide the fields. Joe and Ed were committed to the landing, and once committed with the plane in such bad shape they had no choice but to land.

If we had hit that rock fence head on, we'd have been in trouble. But our pilot and co-pilot, with miraculous strength and Divine Help, set the tail of the airplane down in front of the wall causing the plane to bounce over the wall and belly-land on the other side. Because the systems had been shot out we had no hydraulics and weren't able to lower the landing gear and that was probably a good thing. Our wheels may have hit the wall on the way over and we might have crashed nose down in the soft soil with who knows what harm to the crew.

The landing was a solid bump and we skewed sideways to a dusty stop. I've got to say I've had rougher wheels-down landings on paved runways. I don't think we skidded more than 150 feet. Those pilots did a fantastic job and made a landing we could all walk away from.

1.
MY EARLY DAYS

I grew up in Massillon, Ohio, born in May, 1918. My earliest memory is of a house on State Street, a big house with an attic and a basement. The basement had a coal-fired furnace. The fire door had a sliding grille to adjust draft on the firebox. One day, alone in the basement, I took a straw from a broom, stuck it through the grille and it caught fire. I dropped it on a stack of newspapers and that started a blaze.

Mother had just come looking for me, saw what had happened, and called the Fire Department. Their response was immediate. To a three year-old, those firemen looked huge in their water repellant gear. They scared me more than had the fire. They gave me a stern lecture before leaving. My family had quite a cleanup job.

The family moved from State Street to Greenville, Ohio, just east of Massillon. Greenville was a rural community with unpaved roads and boardwalks. It boasted a jitney, a streetcar on rails that came from Massillon. Fare for riding the jitney was a nickel.

We lived next to a Baptist church and we'd often see worshippers arrive by horse and buggy, or occasionally riding bareback.

Playing outside one day, I found a penny and made tracks for the grocery store across the street. I stepped from the boardwalk onto the road and got hit by a man test-driving a new car. I suffered a cut to my head—the driver decided not to buy the car. That was in 1922 when I was four years old.

My older brothers, Gail and Glenn, decided that for entertainment Eleanor Patterson (also four) and I should get married. Mother made me a wedding shirt from one of my dad's worn out ones. Brother Gail acted as the preacher and Glenn served as my best man. All the kids in Greenville witnessed the ceremony. After the wedding we had cake and lemonade. Later came the ritual "belling," with all the kids gathering around our house and making all the noise they could until called home for bedtime.

We moved back to Massillon and rented a house on Main Street at Wisner, a big house with a big yard. By that time we had a mixed-breed black dog, a lovable family pet. Whatever game we happened to be playing, he was part of it.

Not long after that, the local automobile dealer enlisted my dad's help in driving new cars from the factory in Pontiac, Michigan, to Massillon. While in Michigan on one of those trips, Dad learned that jobs were plentiful in Flint. The Great Depression had just begun and Dad's jobs in the steel industry were drying up.

In 1927, when I was nine years old, our family moved to Flint, Michigan, and I stayed in that area until joining the service. My dad found plenty of work, moving from job to job, though not in the steel industry.

My parents never owned a house; we always rented and in some interesting, different places. At one place, a neighbor, Francie Friend, had a fenced-in chicken yard where fowl could roam free. Francie had a chicken coop in the back yard and nesting boxes where chickens laid their eggs. Among her chickens she had a Bantam rooster, or "Banty" to us kids. That blamed rooster singled me out for an attack every time I entered the yard. My brothers could enter at will and were never a target of that bird. But the Banty would fly at me, wings flapping, and peck at my head. Everyone laughed about it, except me.

In the 1930's, there were two high schools in Flint: Northern High School and Central High School. A good friend that I worked with after graduating had a girl cousin who went to Central High—I had gone to Northern—and he got us together. When I say I married my high school sweetheart that really isn't an accurate statement since we went to different schools and even graduated in different years.

I was two years older than my wife-to-be and had been working at Chevrolet and going to school at night before we met. We were married after she got out of high school.

My job with Chevrolet then was in what they called the Parts Department, a warehousing operation. When orders for car parts came in from dealers, we would fill them from a warehouse in Flint.

I transferred to the National Order Department where we worked from an inventory control system that helped us have on-hand in the warehouse any part any Chevrolet dealer might need to service a customer's car. We placed orders with suppliers and followed them through to delivery to keep our inventories current with demand.

I started working for Chevrolet in 1936. By 1941, the war was looming. I saw an article in the paper saying that the government needed people who had certain, precise skills. They were describing *exactly* what I was doing at Chevrolet! I talked it over with my family—I had a young son by then, Bob, just two years old—and decided I'd offer the military my services. I figured I'd be in an office somewhere in the United States and thought I might be able to control my destiny by volunteering to do for Uncle Sam what I was doing for my company. I never imagined that I'd be pressed into combat.

In October, 1942, I applied and soon got my "welcome letter" from the Army. A bus carried several of us inductees to the Cadillac Building in Detroit where we were formally sworn into the Army after performing and passing physicals. Events immediately following my induction are a bit foggy in my mind, involving a myriad of temporary posts, but I'll reconstruct them to the best of my ability.

From Michigan the Army sent me to Kentucky, a base or city that's lost in the dark reaches of my mind. I don't even recall how I got there. Kentucky was just a staging area. They brought in recruits from all over and then shipped them out to various other locations. We had a few days with nothing to do—until the NCOs noticed and corrected that deficiency. As an officer candidate, they had me assigning KP to other soldiers, which was okay since that meant I didn't have to pull KP myself. That only lasted two days before I got shipped out again.

From there I went to another station whose name and location also escape me. That would have been in December 1942. I got permission to go home because my dad had died. The Red Cross provided me a railroad ticket to home from wherever I was stationed.

When I returned from bereavement leave, the Army then ordered me back to Michigan, to a clearing station at Fort Custer, near Battle Creek. There they gave my fellow enlistees and me IQ tests. My IQ at that time was 142. We received quite a bit of initial testing to determine where our best aptitudes and abilities lay.

In civilian life, I'd been active in softball and bowling leagues, so I thought I was in pretty good shape. The Army's tests told me I had work to do. The mental tests, without reference books, helped the administering officers place inductees in areas of service compatible with their abilities. While all of these tests were indicative of our individual aptitudes, it wasn't unusual for a recruit to wind up in a field totally unrelated to the talents indicated in the test results.

We were then sent to Camp Croft, South Carolina, near Spartanburg, for basic training or boot camp. We went through quite a bit of intense training there, a lot of it field drilling. Before long, I got the distinct impression that they had overlooked what I had applied for. I went in as a VOC, volunteer officer candidate. That had been stamped on all my papers but they didn't seem to be looking at my papers at all. We were going through basic training to become a heavy weapons company, not exactly what I had in mind.

Only one other time did my VOC status came into play. The lieutenant who led our group assigned me to lead the drill instruction for the company in a field exercise. I had them all over the place. What I was doing was fine, but the troops were marching pretty far from their initial point before I brought them back. I never received any formal feedback on the drill.

That was the second and last time they ever tested me as far as my VOC capabilities were concerned. From that point on, I was on my own. The military didn't pay any attention to the VOC. They were going to put me where they wanted me.

Field drills were many and varied with lots of marching and shooting, as well as simulated combat conditions. One day we were practicing with fixed bayonets, but with the scabbards in place to prevent accidental injury. I had been teamed up with Ben Edwards, a co-worker in civilian life, and there we were facing each other. I had my rifle with scabbard-covered bayonet attached, and we were supposed to simulate an attack. When Ben made his charge toward me, instead of lowering the rifle and pulling the bayonet away, I straightened up and shoved it toward him. He caught the point of the scabbard right under his chin. I hadn't put any force behind it and it didn't leave a mark on him, but it scared the bejeebers out of him. And when I saw what I had done, it scared the hell out of me, too.

Corporal Nadeo, our platoon NCO, vented his displeasure on me. He gave me extra duty in the barracks and, thanks to my efforts, the barracks sparkled.

I had worked with Ben at Chevrolet back in Flint, but he wasn't my brother-in-law, not the guy who introduced me to his cousin who I later married. I can still remember Ben's serial number because it was just one digit higher than mine. His dad was an executive with Chevrolet and worked in Detroit. It's amazing that he and I entered the service together and stayed together for such a long time. We didn't separate until I passed the Air Corps exam.

We attended a lecture one day in the barracks hall, and when the lecture had been completed we were dismissed. As we were rising to leave, a sergeant ran out on the stage and said, "Hey guys, wait a minute, wait a minute! Anyone with an IQ of 110 or better can apply for the Air Corps exam."

The possibility of becoming a flyer sounded exciting to me. While I tried to get my VOC straightened out, I thought I'd better apply for the Air Corps. In a few days I received a notice that there would be an Air Corps Qualification Test coming up and I had been selected to take it. It was about a four-hour exam. I got through with it a little early and went out to the waiting room to pass the time until I got my results.

Soon a corporal came out and yelled my name. I jumped up and went to him fully expecting to have made a good grade. He said, "Sorry, but you failed."

I said, "No way. I aced that damn thing!"

"We can't argue with the results," the corporal insisted. "You failed."

I sat back down feeling really low because I knew in my heart that I had nailed that exam. No question. I *knew* it! I just can't explain what a depressed feeling came over me. I absolutely knew I had aced that dad-blamed test.

I waited for another fellow from my outfit to finish the exam, Ben, the same guy I almost bayoneted a few days earlier.

The corporal came back out all smiles and said to me, "Geez, I'm glad you're still here. We used the wrong key to grade your test."

I had aced that darn thing! Unfortunately, Ben did not pass.

We returned to our unit and wondered what the next step would be.

2.
AVIATOR TRAINING

I stayed with my unit until they could get me transferred to Nashville, Tennessee—I don't recall the name of the post there. The Corps had an evaluation center there where they tested our aptitudes to be pilots, navigators, or bombardiers. We went through a series of tests for everything from hand-eye coordination to a lot of math and physics, all sorts of things. It was a grueling process.

I remember they were having a rainy spell in Nashville. The camp streets were pure mud. With the rain coming down like it was, the streets stayed muddy much of the time. In spite of weather conditions, the barracks had to be clean and shoes polished, both ready for any unannounced inspection.

One of the tests at Nashville involved eye coordination at a distance, a test of depth perception. The device we used in that test had a string that we used to move a peg, trying to align it with another, stationary peg some distance away. I stopped the peg where I thought it was next to the other peg, and the NCO who ran the test asked me to do it again. He had me repeat the test five times. He said, "I've seldom seen better depth perception!" It was good to learn that my eyes seemed to be in good shape

When the evaluation had been completed, I qualified for all three specialties: pilot, navigator, and bombardier. The evaluation board decided that I should be a pilot. I couldn't believe my good fortune because that's exactly what I wanted. I can remember telling my ninth grade teacher that I wanted to be an airline pilot.

We were going through basic Air Corps training when they pulled eight of us out of a class of around 40 and said they were going to make us bombardier/navigators. The schools were running a bit behind and they weren't graduating men fast enough to meet the demand for those specialties overseas.

While disappointed to be pulled out of pilot training, at least I'd still be in the Air Corps.

Returning pilots, navigators, and bombardiers who had completed their quota of missions overseas were now assigned as teachers. They told us of a significant loss in those aviation specialties, due to combat casualties as well as meeting mission quotas. I had no idea what a mission quota was and wouldn't even think of the term again until I'd been in combat for a while. Not all of those returning aviators were anxious to return to combat, but some were and that inspired us.

There wasn't a class available for bombardiers just then, so the other air candidates and I had an interim where we weren't studying and weren't taking tests. After three or four days, the Corps didn't know what to do with us until a school became available, so they sent us to Santa Ana, California. That's in southern California, the San Diego area.

We were there for maybe six weeks. That would have been in late 1942. Aside from military classes, I recall that there was a nearby airship hangar that interested me quite a bit. Flying in one of those things was something I'd always wanted to do. The dirigible, blimp, or whatever it was called was on duty, performing daily patrols for submarines off the coast. Several of us wanted to ride along, but they wouldn't take us. That would have been strictly against protocol.

Whenever there is a group of military men in one place, they'll be playing a game of some kind before long. We played a lot of poker. In one particular session, one of the fellows and I butted heads a number of times on different hands. Each time I won. He was not happy. About the time we planned a pretty good-size game, they called to transport us to our next location. They put us on different trains with different destinations and we never got to finish our feud at the poker table. My rival was upset that he couldn't get a chance for his revenge.

From Santa Ana, they sent us to Monroe, Louisiana, where we finally began aviation training. We had regular classes and plenty of homework. One of our instructors there was a Navy lieutenant, junior grade, an O-2. He was a good instructor. Of all the things he taught us, I remember parts of a poem he read to us in class one day. The weather in Monroe was very cold and the poem reflected that:

"Kee-rist but it's cold in Monroe, colder than the nipple on a witch's ...,
"Colder than a pile of penguin ....
''Kee-rist but it's cold in Monroe, colder than the rim of a cocktail glass,
"Colder than the hair on a polar bear's ...''

I won't go any further than that because it gets pretty rough. A lot of barracks language had to be unlearned upon return to civilian life

The LT taught us artillery, among other subjects. That seemed strange, him being in the Navy, but he was an artillery expert. I probably didn't realize it at the time, but many Navy ships had some very large guns on them and naval expertise in artillery was legendary. I still have pictures I drew of some of the things he explained to us.

The Lieutenant told us, too, that at that particular time there were only 11 bomb disposal experts in the US military. I thought that might be a good expertise to have, not much competition for promotion, so I began questioning him about it.

He discouraged the heck out of me. "That's not something you want to get into," he warned, adding that the bomb disposal field is by nature "self-limiting."

I gave it up on his advice, but probably would have changed my mind anyhow.

The first B-17 bomber I ever saw was parked on the runway preparing for takeoff from Selman Field near Monroe. It looked huge. A DC-3 took off before him. The DC-3 had climbed probably not more than 150-200 feet when it suddenly plummeted back to earth. The field was closed down immediately and we never did learn what had happened. There had to be serious injuries, but I don't know how many or how severe they were.

The DC-3 that crashed was a military version, not a commercial airliner. That plane was and still is used for many different applications. For example, they're used for troop transport, cargo, and even as gunships. Puff the Magic Dragon, the gunship capable of such withering fire during the Vietnam War, was a converted DC-3. Many smaller countries still use DC-3s as their main passenger carrier. I've ridden in several that were set up for passengers. Those used by the military for troop transport were bare-bones, no insulation, web seating, and so forth.

We went from Monroe to Coral Gables, Florida, the University of Miami. There we went through an extensive navigation training program. When I say extensive, I mean it. It was in depth. We learned a whole lot about stars, galaxies, and weather, meteorology being a major portion of what we studied. I think the reality of what we were being trained for was so ingrained in the instructors that we may have gone to a deeper level in some of those classes than you would normally expect in a college course. It was tough, really hard.

UofM was an interesting place to be. Not only was the area scenic, a very pretty place, but the camaraderie there was just great. There were special courses for us, run by military instructors and some civilians. I remember that our meteorology instructor was a civilian and he was terrific. He was a short fellow with a very pleasant teaching style that informed but held us accountable for learning.

We also learned to use a sextant while flying on a PBY, an amphibious plane sometimes called a flying boat. PBYs normally flew coastal patrol missions and could stay aloft for hours. On one training flight in a PBY, I was surprised at the amount of space the plane had. Eight of us cadets with our navigation maps and gear had plenty of room to do our job. We only used the sextant on one flight and that one had been preplanned by the instructors to give us experience. If I were to be given a sextant today, I wouldn't be able to use it. I just don't remember the things we were looking for and how we'd set the device.

One of the major advances at that point was the E6B computer, a round slide rule apparatus, sometimes called a "whiz wheel." It had a slide in it with longitude and latitude markings, which slid under a Plexiglas face that had degrees marked on it that we treated as a compass. Using a marker, we could actually plot a full course on the face of that s E6B. We could take into consideration such things as wind direction and airspeed, just like on a regular flight but we were doing it on a hand-held device. Really an interesting gadget and they're still around today. In fact, I have one among my souvenirs.

We had class after class on hypothetical cases. We'd draw charts and plot courses that involved all kinds of weather conditions, making adjustments on our flight plans for whatever changes there were. We learned to read waves on the ocean through the Norden bombsight. If you looked through the glass and knew what you were looking for, you could determine the wind direction and even estimate the wind speed at the surface.

The sight was an optical device with crosshairs. The crosshairs represented the course of the aircraft (direction of flight toward the target) and the rate (rate of speed approaching the target). We put into the bombsight such things as airspeed, true airspeed, ground speed, altitude, temperature, wind direction, and humidity. All that information we dialed into the bombsight. As I dialed those things in, the course line might change and then I'd make corrections to compensate. The object was to get the course line centered over the target. The same thing happened with the rate line, so we had to adjust our speed to make the course and rate lines hold steady and bisect directly over the target.

Here's where the hard-to-believe stuff comes in: When the course line was holding steady on the target and all conflicting factors had been removed, we'd center the rate line on the target by adjusting the speed of the plane. At that point the magic of the sight took over and, when its internal computations matched the cross hairs, bombs were released automatically. The trick was to get neither of the lines to move at all, just let the plane fly over the target. The bombsight gave us the best indicator as to when the bombs should be released. When we got the course line and the rate line to center over the target and stay there, then we stopped adjustments. When the sight did its thing, the bombs were automatically away.

The bombsight was amazing in that it mechanically calculated all the things needed to hit the target. It took into account the speed of the plane, the altitude, the drop angle of the bombs, everything. I say this with tongue in cheek, but the Norden bombsight was the GPS of its time. It was the ultimate advance in bombing technique.

Development of the bombsight originated many years before WWII. A fellow named Sperry came up with an earlier sight that didn't go quite as far as Norden's version. But, with many refinements, the Sperry device served as the basis for the Norden bombsight. There was another device made by Raytheon, I think. Norden took those basic sights and added his refinements, improving the device tremendously. The result was superb.

We'd set the course line, and then plug in speed and all the other information. We'd look at the target through the bombsight. We'd set up in advance of the drop point and, when we got there, the lead bombardier relied on his input into the sight to allow for the sight to automatically release his bombs. When his bombs dropped, the rest of us dropped our bombs, too, regardless of what our bombsights said. His bombs were aimed dead center on the target and the bombs from the rest of us would be spread out from there.

When we got into practical training, they put us in a PBY, flying down fairly close to the surface of the ocean. Most of our navigation just followed the shoreline. We did some off-shore flying, navigating a preplanned route in search of enemy subs.

A couple of things about Florida—we were in Coral Gables, a beautiful place. We lived in Sebastian Hall, a male dormitory at the university. We marched almost daily to the Vesuvius Swimming Pool, a beautiful pool, for exercise and recreation. It was rock-lined and a huge rock served as one of the diving platforms. I think it was a manmade rock, but artistically made and it looked like we were diving off a big rock into the pool.

One evening several of us went out on the town. We were supposed to be back at the dorm by 10 pm and the cab driver assured us we'd get there in time, but we got hung up in traffic. We punched in at 10:01, one minute late. As a result, we were called before the disciplinary board. The board assigned us to walk tours as punishment. That amounted to marching with a full pack for four hours on a short, circular track. It was only about 35 steps around the track. Once the four-hour tour was over, that was it. Our debt had been paid.

Another thing I remember about Coral Gables: It seemed to rain at three o'clock every afternoon.

Three classmates and I stayed in a room with four double bunks; mine was an upper bunk. We were always supposed to stretch our blanket tightly over the bed when we made it. Whenever the orderly on duty came through, he'd flip a quarter on the bed. If the quarter didn't bounce, we had to remake the bed.

I got the bright idea that I'd sleep on top of my blanket and not mess up my bed. In Florida I didn't need to sleep under a blanket; my bath towel was just fine. The next morning, I'd just tuck the blanket in real tight. The quarter always bounced on my bed.

Toward the end of navigation training, they pulled seven of us out of class to go to bombardier training. The reports from overseas didn't make it sound like such a bad turn of events. We'd been hearing that navigators were being popped off frequently, killed at a high rate, especially those coming out of Britain. So we thought maybe being a bombardier wouldn't be so bad. Come to think of it, navigators and bombardiers are on the same plane—so much for clear-thinking cadets!

Bombardier schools were full, so they made the decision to send us to an air-to-air gunnery school at McCarran Field near Las Vegas, Nevada—McCarran Field is now the main commercial airport for the city. Let me tell you a couple of stories about that:

The Flamingo Hotel/Casino was the newest and located on what then seemed to be the edge of town. Now it's right downtown. The Golden Nugget was there, too, and there were others but I don't recall their names. We managed to get into town occasionally, usually on weekends.

A group of us went into Las Vegas one evening and found our way to the Flamingo. We didn't have a lot of money, obviously, but we got to playing on a crap table. One of the cadets in our group did the shooting and I decided to bet on him. He'd make a relatively sizable bet and I'd make a much smaller one. He won something over $2500 that night, and I won about $200. I thought I had cashed in, but he really did well.

There were civilian clientele at the casino and quite a few military, too. At a bank of slot machines—I don't remember the denominations—an elderly woman played one of the machines. She cranked the lever on that one-armed bandit like you wouldn't believe. In those days, the casinos didn't have people with trays coming around to make change for the gamblers, at least I don't recall there being any. I think gamblers had to go to the cashier for change. The elderly lady left her machine and went to the cashier to get more tokens, quarters, or whatever. By the time she got back, there was a man playing her machine. She beat the fool out of him with her purse. The poor guy didn't know what he had done. She was livid because he had taken *her* machine. She had primed it and now he was playing it. He was a great sport about it, laughing while she beat him with her purse. The security people handled the situation very quietly and everyone parted friends.

While we were at McCarran, we took an awful lot of training, including air-to-air firing from an open-cockpit AT-6. In air-to-air firing, another plane would go up with a towed target behind it, really just a big sock, like a windsock at the airport. We had .50-caliber machineguns aboard our planes and that's what we used to shoot at the target. All of our ammunition had been coated in paint. My ammo might have been dipped in red paint, while the next guy's might have been dipped in blue or green. That way, instructors could tell who hit the target and who missed. One plane would make a pass at the target, with the gunner shooting. Then another plane would make a pass, and so on.

One day I fired ahead of the target, trying to lead it, and accidentally clipped the tow wire. The sock went floating off into the distance. We couldn't see the pilot of the tow plane then, but when we got back on the ground he was livid. He said, "As long as I've been doing this, nobody had ever clipped the tow wire."

He was not a happy camper. At first I didn't understand it, but eventually realized that he had to go back up with another target for another flyer to shoot at, instead of getting some coveted downtime. In Army terms, he was "pissed off."

That story makes me sound like a champion shooter, someone who's done something no one else has done, but that's not the case at all. It was purely by accident that I clipped the wire towing the target. I had no intention of doing that, none at all. I just led the target a bit too much and shouldn't have been firing that far ahead.

On my first such flight at McCarran, the pilot who took me up asked, "Have you ever been in an open-cockpit plane before?" I hadn't.

He said, "Oh. Have you ever been airsick?" I hadn't.

He said, "You will be!"

He was right. I shot at a target, firing from the AT-6 airplane. The machine gun and controls were on a turret mounted in the rear cockpit with the pilot in the front one. I waggled the gun to signal to the pilot that I had finished firing. When he peeled off, he just let the plane drop like a rock, leaving my stomach about 10 feet above my head. Holy Moses, did I get sick!

My wife and my son Bob, he was about three at the time, came to visit me in Las Vegas. They had an interesting episode on the way out there. Flint, Michigan, where they lived was an integrated town. But, for whatever reason, Bob had never seen a black person. A black lady on the train with them had two black children, one of them a little boy about Bob's age. Bob kept looking at him and finally said to him, "Hello, Blackie."

I don't know what else transpired after that, but the mothers got along fine, making nothing of Bob's comment. Bob was just intrigued with the black boy.

I was in Las Vegas when I got my commission as a second lieutenant, in January, 1944. Until then I had been an air cadet, the equivalent of a private first class or E-3.

After about three months in Las Vegas, we were transferred to Carlsbad, New Mexico, for bombardier school. We went through extensive training on mapping courses and doing plot-work. We also did a lot of flying, including at night. Whenever we returned from a night flight, the KPs would have a light snack waiting for us, ham-and-cheese sandwiches for example. They had some pretty good food, including desserts that were not only very good but plentiful.

Carlsbad brought on several interesting events. On one occasion, one of the field personnel, an enlisted man, asked if he could go along on a night flight. We asked the pilot and the pilot said, "Sure, bring him along."

We were flying an AT-11 Beechcraft, a twin-engine, twin-tail training aircraft. Right ahead of the navigator's table was a cover on the floor held in place by four Zeus fasteners. We could remove the cover and expose an aperture in which we could mount a camera. That was similar to the arrangement we had on our actual mission aircraft, the B-25. We'd mount a camera in the aperture to record the results of our bombing missions. That was a very effective way of determining our success, especially at night. The targets were marked with lighted crosshairs and very often we'd see the center section of the target obliterated.

Anyway, we were up for several hours in the AT-11— we had to have a certain number of hours in flight before we could get our commissions and graduate. During that flight, we did a number of different things not on the flight plan. Eventually, someone thought about the young man off the ground crew. We found him at the back of the airplane where the bombardier would normally sit. That night we didn't have a camera onboard. The kid had taken the plate off the aperture and was vomiting through that hole. He was so sick, really in bad shape.

Another time, we were flying at night just to get our hours in, weren't on any mission or anything, just in the air to put in the required time. As we flew along, the plane suddenly made a very noticeable dive and everyone got thrown up against the ceiling. Two planes had almost collided. Pilots are trained on what to do in such situations: One goes up and the other goes down. They did the right thing and we missed each other.

Shortly after that, the Air Corps sent us to B-25 training school in Greenville, South Carolina. While we were there, we were assigned to a crew so we could train with the same people all the time and be familiar with each other by the time we went overseas. We needed to be a well-oiled team. My original crew included LT Harvey Linebarrier and LT Hal Moore (no relation to the Vietnam War hero, as far as I can tell). Both were younger than I but with equal times in service. Our valued NCO crew was comprised of SGT E.H. McConaughy, engineer/gunner; SGT B.B. Plotkin, radioman/waist gunner; and SGT D.W. Sanders, tail gunner.

We did quite a bit of air-to-air and air-to-ground bombardier training. On the latter, we learned all about the Norden bombsight. Later, when we were overseas and took the bombsight from the supply room to the airplane, we walked with a loaded .45 pistol in one hand and the Norden in the other. When we reached the plane we took the bombsight out of its case and attached it to the floor. Then we put our pistols away. The Norden bombsight was a highly classified device and we guarded it carefully.

The instructors on the bombsight were a proficient group of people. They were soldiers, military personnel, and they really knew their business. The head of the group was a captain and the rest were lieutenants and non-coms (non-commissioned officers).

We trained on a scaffold built on wheels, about eight feet above the floor. On top of the scaffold was an actual Norden bombsight, so we were training with the real McCoy. We had the same kind of instruction when we were at Carlsbad, in fact more there than any other place. Using that trainer, we could simulate a whole course of attack, including time, airspeed, temperature, altitude, and the whole business. It didn't matter if the course of attack was two hours, four hours, or whatever, we could simulate the whole thing.

The bug (actually a box on very low wheels, but we called it a bug) on the floor would do whatever we told it to do through the bombsight. When the vertical and horizontal crosshairs lined up, a plunger inside the bug would drop down and make a mark on a piece of paper lying on the floor to tell us exactly where our bomb would have hit. The paper itself was about letter-size, with concentric circles drawn on it. The center circle was our target, a perfect hit if we could make the bug put a mark there. The whole process was an exact replica of what we did in a plane during actual combat. It was a really fine training procedure.

We had a similar instrument in Corsica when we got there, but the floor there was way too rough, about like a corrugated roof, so the training was worthless. We couldn't make the bug do what we wanted it to do. I can't imagine why they didn't have something better.

At low level, the Norden bombsight couldn't be used. It just wasn't possible to get all the necessary information into the computer in time to fire. So they taught us how to use a little pronged instrument for low-level bombing, kind of like a tuning fork but with three tines. I would swear the fork was made of wood, at least that's how I remember it. The bombardier would brace his hand holding the sight against the Plexiglas nose of the airplane. With a little practice sighting over the fork at the target, it was a surprisingly accurate instrument for low level bombing. The bombardier would rely on his intellect and the fork would tell him when to release the bomb.

We became very proficient with that screwy little instrument. We did what we called "skip bombing," where the target would sit vertically on a float in the ocean. We could sight the target over the tines and drop the bomb with reasonable accuracy. It was a simple gadget, like the sights on a rifle. We would approach with the target facing us. If we did as we had been trained, using the fork, we could hit the target with regularity. If we released the bomb too early, it would skip off the water and, hopefully, hit the target, kind of like skipping a stone across the water. Hitting too short wasn't good—sometimes the bomb would sink before reaching the target.

That was a fun experiment. The simulated bombs we used were 100-pound bombs, the same weight as the ones we'd been using on our training flights. The bombs had just enough explosive to give off a flash so we'd know where we had hit.

We didn't have too much training on this procedure, probably because they didn't expect us to do much low-level bombing. That method was intended more for fighter planes. One of the newly-commissioned bombardiers who'd had fair success with the low-level gadget convinced a fighter pilot to let him show off his expertise. When flight time came, the bombardier backed down—he hadn't thought about being in the back seat and not in the nose of the plane. The pilot said he didn't need the "toy" in the first place, that he could be accurate without it.

During training, we dropped our bombs from altitudes between eight thousand and 12 thousand feet, the same as we expected to do in combat. To graduate, we had to have a score of less than 250 in what they called "circular error." In other words, your average bomb had to drop within a 250 foot diameter of the target. My average was 108, so my bombs typically would land within 54 feet of dead center.

I thought I was pretty good. I was so proud of my 108 circular error rating, until I got around a bunch of guys who were running in the 75 to 80 foot range, and some less than that. Those guys were tweaking good!

The lead bombardiers in most squadrons usually had an average circular error not more than two digits. Their 65s, 70s, and 80s made my 108 look paltry. I never served as a lead bombardier because other guys had better circular error statistics than I did, but I flew in the first echelon a number of times.

We relied on the lead bombardier to drop his bombs at precisely the right moment. When he opened his bomb bay doors, everyone in the flight opened theirs, too. When he released his bombs, so did everyone else. When our planes hit the IP, the Initial Point, the lead pilot transferred control of the aircraft to his bombardier. From then on until the bombs were released, for about 30 seconds, the bombardier controlled the plane through the Norden bombsight. All the other bombardiers had their sights zeroed on the target and ready to go in the event something happened to the lead plane, but otherwise we all dropped our loads manually when the leader dropped his bombs.

One day while we were in Greenville, we marched in formation out to a parade ground near our quarters. The Army had arranged a flyover of six B-25s, three-by-three. Immediately over us, one of the planes clipped the tail of one of the other planes. There were pieces of fuselage falling like leaves from the sky. One of the planes crashed and the other crash-landed. All six members of the first crew and an onboard observer died. That happened immediately before we got into the final phase of training and went overseas. It started bringing things into perspective for us.

The observer on the plane that crashed had just come back from overseas. He had completed his missions and had gone along on that flight just as an observer. Imagine, flying numerous combat missions overseas without serious incident, only to be killed after coming back to the States and flying on what should have been a lark flight.

On a night training mission, just before we went overseas, our flight plan took us near Linebarrier's home town in Alabama, just outside Birmingham. He had already called his parents and told them to be ready because he was coming. We buzzed his home. As we approached his home, we had our landing lights on so his parents would know it was us. I looked out the nose of the plane and noticed that we were headed directly for the town's water tower. I screamed into the mike, "Line! Tower!" I always called him "Line." He immediately veered and we took off. If he had reacted just a few seconds later, it could have been disastrous.

Speaking of nights stateside, when the sun went down the lights came on, but they were toned down and shades were pulled. We were 100 miles out, yet we could see the glow of Birmingham. They had their iron foundries going and the glow made the city a perfect target if there had been any enemy bombers in the area.

There was a shortage of housing on the base at Greenville. Toward the end of our stay there, in late April or early May, they allowed married officers to live off-base in town. Some of us stayed at the Wade Hampton Hotel which is gone now. It was a landmark, at least for me.

We arrived in Greenville the end of January, 1944. In early May we got our orders to go overseas, and we were ecstatic. We'd been through all the training and were ready to go. My VOC deal was out the window; I was never going to be an order interpreter for the military as I had imagined before entering the service. Instead, here I was, going overseas and leaving my family behind.

U. S. Army Air Forces

Pre-Flight School
Bombardier - Navigator

Be it known that

Erwin E. Carman

has satisfactorily completed the course of instruction

prescribed for

Pre-Flight Training

at the

A. A. F. Pre-Flight (Bombardier-Navigator) School

In testimony whereof and by virtue of vested authority

I do confer upon him this

DIPLOMA

Given at Selman Field, Louisiana, this __nineteenth__ *day*

of __March__ *in the year of our Lord one thousand nine*

hundred and __forty-three__ .

Attest

Major, A. C.
Director of Training

Major, A. C.
Adjutant

Major, A. C.
Commanding

United States Army
Air Forces
Bombardier School

Be it known that

Aviation Student Erwin Eugene Carman, 36635887

Has satisfactorily completed the course of instruction
PRESCRIBED FOR

Aircraft Observer Bombardier

at Carlsbad Army Air Field, Carlsbad, New Mexico
In Testimony Whereof and by Virtue of Vested Authority

I DO CONFER UPON HIM THIS

Diploma

Given at A.A.F.B.S., Carlsbad, New Mexico this Fifteenth day
of   January   in the year of our Lord one thousand
nine hundred and Forty four

Attest:

_____   _____

HERBERT ROSENTHAL,   J. P. RYAN,
Major, Air Corps,   Colonel, Air Corps,
Director of Training   Commanding

3.
GOING OVERSEAS

The military was so secretive. They didn't want us to know where we were going until we were airborne. When we got off the ground, we couldn't wait to open our orders and see what they said. We learned we were going to Corsica, an island in the Mediterranean just west of Italy and not too far from the coast of France. None of us had ever been to Corsica or anywhere near it and we were all thrilled to know that's where we'd be going.

Maybe I screwed up, saying that the military was so secretive. I don't mean it in a derogatory manner. They *were* secretive. But if we knew where we were going while still on the ground, one of us may have let it slip. The Navy folks always said, "Loose lips sink ships." I'm sure the Air Corps had a corollary, but I don't know what it was.

Our flight overseas began in Greenville, South Carolina, and our first stop was Homestead in south Florida, below Miami and just above the Keys. We had several test flights in Greenville before we took off to get us familiar with the airplane we'd be flying overseas and in combat.

Our next stop was on the western coast of Puerto Rico maybe 200 miles west of San Juan. We landed at what had been a civilian airport, Barinquen Field, a pretty terminal.

We were sitting on a large patio outside the terminal the afternoon we arrived, actually sitting on a low wall that enclosed the patio. We were having drinks and off in the distance we could watch the sun set into the ocean. It was such a sight, just this huge, huge orange ball sinking into the ocean.

HEADQUARTERS
XII Tactical Air Command, Adv
APO #374, U. S. Army

AG 300.3   22 August 1944

SUBJECT: Orders

TO   : Whom it may concern

1. The following named officers and EM WP by mil
acft o/a 22 August 1944 from this station to Hq. Twelfth
Air Force RUAT to A2 section for further disposition.
TDN No funds involved:

1st Lt. Joe W. Maywald, O-761606, AC,
2nd Lt. Erwin E. Carman, O-765466, AC,
F/O Edmund C. Weaver, T-1874, USA,
T/Sgt. Richard R. Mackowiak, 36258813,
S/Sgt. John C. Sequinz, 16132901.

By command of Brigadier General SAVILLE:

C. M. KERANEN,
1st Lt. Air Corps,
Actg. Asst Adj. General.

R-E-S-T-R-I-C-T-E-D

My Overseas Orders

We flew as directly as possible from one stop to the next. We often had to make corrections because a changing wind had blown us off course.

From Puerto Rico we went to Georgetown, British Guiana, on the northern coast of South America. We landed in the middle of a jungle. It was like they had taken a big razor and scraped down through it to clear space for a runway. There were trees on both sides and at both ends of the runway, leaving just this path through the trees. As we got over the trees and were headed for the runway, I saw the most brilliantly colored macaws in the trees. Scads of them, just bunches of them. It was awe-inspiring to see all that color. Beautiful!

The next morning, from Georgetown we flew southeast along the coast of South America until we got to Belém, at the mouth of the Amazon River. We could see all the way across the delta, at least from the air, and it was huge. The silt from the river formed a fan way out into the ocean, a lighter brown area in contrast to the darker colors elsewhere.

Linebarrier was our pilot and he dropped us down pretty low, not exactly following the flight plan. For better communications during our flight, we had a trailing antenna hanging off the bottom of our plane. On the end of the wire was a lead ball to give it ballast that stretch the wire out. We were making a pretty low pass over the delta when I remembered the antenna. I reeled that thing in pretty fast, once I realized what was happening. I pushed a button and an electric motor reeled in the antenna before we snagged something on the ground.

There were dozens of tiny islands in the delta and there were huts built on stilts on many of those little islands. The stilts kept the houses out of the water during rough weather. Their huts on those islands, or aits, were made of bamboo, reeds, or something like that. It looked like cornstalks but probably wasn't. I'll never forget, as we flew across the delta, all the people on those small islands shook their fists at us. They had cattle standing knee-deep in the water and the roar of those B-25 engines did not have a calming effect on them.

I had my first avocado in Belém. The waitress at the mess hall, a Brazilian girl, was anxious to please and very helpful with our orders. When she asked me if I wanted an avocado, I told her I had never had one. She said I'd love it. She brought one, showed me how to cut the fruit, and then brought a special kind of oil to drizzle on it. I'll swear it's one of the best things I've ever eaten. It was a ripe avocado, right off the tree, really excellent. Every time I get a guacamole salad, dip, or anything of the sort, it brings back memories of Belém.

We refueled at Belém, stayed there overnight, and then took off for Natal, Brazil. Natal is southeast of Belém, on the eastern-most tip of South America. Again, we refueled and stayed overnight before taking off for Ascension Island.

As we flew across the ocean, we could see nothing but water in every direction. That gave some of us a better understanding of just how big an ocean is.

Ascension Island is a dot in the middle of the Atlantic Ocean, a very small dot, about halfway between South America and Africa. Several things I remember about Ascension Island:

First, you'd better be flying at the correct altitude when you hit the runway because there's nothing but rock at the beginning of it. At the other end, there's nothing but rock and birds. They had tried everything they could think of to scare off the birds: shotgun blasts, explosions, nets, but nothing worked. The birds kept coming back. Every once in a while they'd lose an airplane because of birds hitting the engines, so we were told. They were huge birds, like ravens. I have no idea what kind they were and I never saw them anywhere else. No one ever told me what they were. They may have been ravens but I'm just not sure.

Second, one of the fellows on an earlier flight was getting ready to leave Ascension Island when we got there. He had a monkey, a little fellow, not much more than six inches high. The monkey was sick; I think it had a cold. Somehow, the guy talked me into taking the monkey because he couldn't take it with him where he was going. But then I had to get rid of it for the same reason because we were leaving the next morning. Somewhere in our training or briefings, we'd been told we couldn't take animals from one country to another. I was gung-ho as a novice airman and abided by all the rules, a go-by-the-book guy. Luckily, I found another lieutenant to take the monkey.

On Ascension Island we had wooden barracks for quarters. In all other cases en route to Corsica, we slept in tents. We refueled the plane and stayed overnight at each stop and had little time to sight-see. Looking back, it would have been a great to have had time to explore, however briefly, each of the stops we made but we weren't on a pleasure trip.

The crew with whom I trained and flew to Europe
Kneeling (L-R): Carl Sanders, E. H. McConaughy, B.B. Plotkin
Standing (L-R): Gene Carman, Harold Moore, Harvey Linebarrier,
Instructor M. Hardin

From Ascension Island we flew to the west coast of Africa, the Gold Coast, about the western-most point on that continent. The Ivory Coast is the name of a country, but the Gold Coast is an area encompassing several countries on the west coast of Africa, one of which was Ghana. Gold had been discovered in several locations in western Africa, back around the year 1000, I think. The British arrived just before Columbus sailed for America, and they gave the area its name.

I don't recall how long it took us to fly from Brazil to Ascension Island or from there to Africa, but we made each leg during daylight. We left at dawn and got to the next point before sundown, sometimes by mid-afternoon. That's the way it went for each leg of our trip, not just the ones over the ocean. Each leg of our trip lasted on the order of six to eight hours.

Our landing spot there was Accra, the capital of Ghana. As we landed, there stood one of the blackest black men I've ever seen. As we taxied to the end of the runway on landing, that's where we first saw him. We turned around and taxied to the parking area some distance away, and by the time we got there he was there, too. How in the devil he got that far that fast I don't know. He was an older gentleman so I don't know how he could have moved that quickly.

He was one of the first civilians we had run into on our trip overseas. He was stripped to the waist, wearing just shorts. There's just no nice way to say this, but his testicles were hanging out of his shorts. His feet looked like they were six inches wide—huge feet.

He was a story teller, but none of his stories were true. We had heard that there were huge snakes in Africa, and asked him about it. He said, "Oh yeah, there was one out here just the other day. It caught a fellow by the leg and had that leg all gobbled up by the time we got to him. They had to amputate his leg, but they saved him."

That was an absolute, pure falsehood, but he told it convincingly. He could tell the strangest tales and with a straight face. If somebody called him on it, he'd just smile. He'd tell stories with emotion and passion, and we'd believe every word he said until he got to a certain point, at which he'd give himself away. He'd kind of smile. His command of the English language was exceptional and, with a heavy accent, delightful.

It was hot there, oh gosh it was hot.

The next morning when I got out of my cot, I picked up my shoes from under the bed. Somewhere in my training I had been told to shake out my shoes before putting them on. I did that and, sure enough, there was a big centipede in one of them. Whether or not he was the kind that would sting I couldn't say, but he was in my shoe. I'm sure I would have felt him if I'd just put my foot in it.

Later, as I sat on a rock wall outside the tent complex, a movement on the ground caught my eye. I looked up and saw the biggest spider I had ever seen moving toward me. It had spectacular black coloring with brilliant, yellow trim. Its eyes were on what looked like poles sticking out of its head. For a minute I couldn't move, just fascinated by this crazy creature. He came toward me, probably not to attack, but I didn't hang around to find out.

From Accra we flew north to Dakar, the capital of Senegal. The most memorable thing I saw there were the local soldiers. They were such magnificent-looking men. They were all dressed in shorts and khaki shirts. They were absolutely beautiful physical specimens, really good-looking body types.

In Corsica, a company of Senegalese soldiers encamped just east of us. That had to be late July, 1944. My crewmate and I were watching one of those soldiers. The fellow had something on the palm of his hand that looked like a leather pad. With his other hand he held a round metal disc, about six inches across that he twisted back and forth across the leather pad. I got the impression he was honing the disc, like you would strop a razor.

When he finished, he took that disc and threw it at a branch on a tree that was maybe 10 yards away from him. The disc hit the branch and cut it from the tree. He polished the disc a little more, and then threw it at another branch with the same results. The accuracy of his throws was really something else. One branch he lopped off with his disc had to be at least an inch across, maybe more.

That event really stuck in my mind. I'm so glad the Senegalese were on our side—they were fearsome looking people. We heard that the Senegalese soldiers later invaded Elba and took the island. There were many Nazi casualties and we wondered if they resulted from discs like the one we'd seen being stropped and thrown.

From Dakar we left for Marrakech. The pilot had been briefed, of course, but I did all the navigating, as I had for the entire trip, for experience and to hone my skills. As we skirted the west coast of Africa heading north, we got to a certain point where my navigational skills were tested. The pilot had been told in pre-flight that he had to "get this right because when you make the final turn you should be looking directly down the valley between the mountains at Marrakech."

Coming up to that turning point, we were flying north from Dakar along the coast of Africa. According to navigational techniques, when we reached that point on our estimated time of arrival, we needed to make a 90-degree turn to the right. As we got close to turn point, Linebarrier, our pilot, called and asked how much further until we make the turn. I told him 35 seconds. When he made his right turn 35 seconds later, we were looking right down that valley. Line called me back and said, "One for you, Gene!"

I don't mean to sound pompous but I'll admit it pleased me to have nailed that navigation problem so accurately. Making good calculations while training in the United States was one thing, but this was a real confidence builder.

At Marrakech, we were not in the city. I didn't see the town itself because I never left the airfield and saw only whatever had sprung up around it. There were a sparse number of buildings, nothing over two stories high, and very few of them. As I remember, all the buildings seemed to be of adobe-type construction. There was dust everywhere, being a desert area. I can't imagine living in that heat permanently.

I remember leaving Marrakech on our way to Tunisia. We were flying at about 8,000 feet. We looked down and could see a dust cloud that must have come up to nearly 6,000 feet, the bottom being on the floor of the Sahara Desert. Looking down from above, we saw the compacted view of the cloud and it looked much denser than it appeared on the ground.

Tunis was the last stop before we reached Ghisonaccia. I can't remember a thing about Tunis, while other locations where we stopped are clear as a bell. I can't figure out what was so different about Tunisia to make it disappear from my memory.

4.
CORSICA

The next day we flew from Tunisia to our final destination: Corsica. On take-off, we flew through another dust cloud, a thick, brown dust. When we got up to our assigned altitude and looked down, we could see that the dust covered the land and must have extended up to about 4,000 feet. We saw dust over the Sahara from a lower angle once we were on Corsica.

We made an overnight stop on each leg of our trip to Corsica. We didn't have to do anything as far as setting up tents. They had been erected for us and all the other flyers en route to the war zones. Ascension Island was the only exception, with barracks in which to stay.

Ghisonaccia was the nearest village to our airfield on Corsica, east of us and on the central coast. We were situated a few miles inland, not far from the foothills. Where the airfield was, we had to be on the outskirts of that city, but I don't remember anybody ever mentioning that they had gone there for entertainment, relaxation, or anything else. Like I said, it was the nearest village, but must have been too small to attract our attention.

Nowadays I hear they have bus tours and car rentals are available, even railroad tours. So, they must have expanded tremendously since the war.

The Island of Corsica

We didn't know it at the time, but there were combat pilots on the ground at Ghisonaccia judging each landing, including ours, as we came in. Our pilot, Linebarrier, was pretty darn good and this time he put down a squeaker. That's a very positive thing. When I say "he squeaked that landing," I mean he did it perfectly as our tires touched, smoked and squeaked. If you've watched the shuttle Discovery make a landing, when the pilot made the tires squeak and the smoke roll, everyone on the ground would applaud a perfect touchdown, as well as the safe return of the space heroes.

The command in Corsica had a policy that an incoming pilot and copilot would be reassigned to another crew with a veteran pilot. One of the pilots watching our landing was a fellow named Lieutenant Lytle. Lytle watched and, when Linebarrier squeaked in our landing, he was impressed. He wanted our pilot to become his copilot. We had some very bouncy landings at times, but Linebarrier really pulled that one off nicely. Lytle knew he wanted the pilot who'd made such a great landing.

Lieutenant Lytle joined us as our pilot and Linebarrier stayed with us as our co-pilot. Hal Moore, our co-pilot in the States and on this overseas flight, got assigned to another crew.

The runway we used near Ghisonaccia was composed of interlocking metal sheets. The sheets, it seemed to me, were eight or 10 feet long, and I'm not too sure about the width, maybe something like three or four feet. As I said, the sheets interlocked, and also had holes in them to facilitate draining in case of rain. When a plane landed on this planking, it was just like landing on a concrete runway. They were fine, worked out great, and saved the engineers a whole lot of trouble and time building runways.

Linebarrier, Hal Moore, and I were quartered together above the mess hall. We had to go up one flight of stairs to a landing, and then up another flight of stairs to the second floor. There was one room up there, quite large and had plenty of space for the three of us. We each had an Army cot against an inner wall of the building with mosquito netting in place. Windows on three walls provided plenty of daylight and air movement.

On the landing between the floors was a large chest with a lock on it. We didn't know it at the time, but that chest housed the base liquor supply. When a crew came back from a mission, a guard would unlock the chest and pass out one serving of liquor to anyone so inclined. After we'd been there for just a few days, I tried a G.I. key I happened to have and I'll be darned if that key didn't open the liquor chest! Of all the millions of locks and keys the Corps must have had, I had just the right key to fit that particular lock. To think that on that liquor chest, a GI key I just happened to have would fit that lock was unthinkable, but it did.

I don't drink now—I did then, but tried not to overdo it. I must admit that once in a while we took advantage of our luck. The guards just couldn't figure out why the liquor supply seemed to be depleting at an unexpected rate.

In another building, we wanted to use the upper level as an officer's club. We had to do a lot of repairing and decorating. Some men in our group were good artists, fine artists really. In a corner of the landing between floors, one of the artists painted a picture of a most voluptuous woman ever. He painted her in the corner of the landing, and right in front of her were imprints on the floor of a man's feet pointing directly toward her. The footprints were positioned so that she couldn't escape and our imaginations could run wild.

When replacement aircraft engines came in from the States, they arrived in rough oak crates. A building near our base had been a milling center, but the milling equipment there hadn't been used in some time. The mill hadn't been destroyed or damaged badly; it had just been abandoned. A bunch of GIs on the base put the mill back together. They cleaned, polished, and lubricated all the machinery and got it working.

Then they took the boards from the rough oak crates and planed them down smooth. Between them and the rest of the crews, they built a lot of furniture. They built some of the most fabulous stuff, like a bar you just wouldn't believe. The artists decorated the wall behind the bar and did great work.

My job had been to build a dice table. We lined the base and side rails with material from GI blankets, nice and smooth, tight as it could be. The artists in our group got busy, painting and carving all sorts of things on the walls. We had a very nice little club when we were done.

Colonel Henson, a visiting observer, had been on the General Doolittle B-25 raid on Tokyo in 1942. He was also a big gambler. When we finished making the craps table, we made a sign to hang over it that said, "Hensen's Waterloo." He got a big kick out of that. That table was well-used.

Outside our mess hall in Ghisonaccia lay a rusted locomotive, a small-gauge steam engine turned on its side. There were no train tracks in the area, so I'm not sure how the locomotive got there. When we got to Corsica, immediately we were given instructions to dig foxholes for ourselves to use in the event of an attack. The Germans were in Italy, right across the water from us. I scouted around near the locomotive and found a hole right under the engine, so I didn't have to dig. I had found my foxhole! I don't know how many other guys found that hole, too, but it probably would have been crowded if we'd all had to get in there.

Once we got established in Corsica, we'd have a movie every two weeks or so. When bombs were shipped to us, there'd be a metal container over the back of each bomb to protect the fins. Those metal containers were about 18 inches tall, just right for seats and that's what we sat on during the movies. We'd go to the movie and get there a little early. Sitting on those metal seats, we would look to the south and see the most beautiful skies across the Mediterranean you could ever imagine.

The sun hitting the dust off the Sahara Desert would put colors in the sky that you couldn't believe, the most beautiful thing imaginable. I wish I could explain it adequately, but I can't. We'd just sit there oohing and aahing. Wind would move the dust and the sun hitting that movement gave us our own Aurora Borealis—constant change with dips and surges—beauty we really enjoyed.

A number of good entertainers came to Corsica with the USO, Pearl Bailey among them. Bob Hope never made it to Corsica while I was there but I did see him when he came to entertain us in Miami after my return to the States.

Once we were settled into our quarters and had the routine fairly well in control, we enjoyed exploring the area around our base. On such an outing in a heavily forested area, we found a clearing with a concrete pad about 12 feet square—just the pad with no structure on it. Lying in the open on that pad was a black powder handgun, which I pounced on. It was in exceptional condition, completely intact. Later, during a cleaning session, I found a wad of paper in the barrel and removed it. Unfortunately, the paper got damaged. There had been French writing on the paper but was no longer decipherable. My son, Randy, has the gun now.

Major Lawrence Hill served as our commander, a real nice guy from Alabama. He called us into formation one day, a thing we hadn't done for some time. So, here we are right off the coast of Italy, which at the time the Germans patrolled frequently. They sent planes over us constantly, reconnaissance flights looking for Allied activity. So, when the Major called a formation in the daytime, I wondered, *What is the matter with his mind?* This happened shortly after we joined the group, and we still expected an enemy behind every rock and tree! In our minds, if the Germans had seen us in formation, we probably would have been attacked soon thereafter! It turned out that he was just following orders. We fell into formation and, as soon as the short formation was over, we dispersed quickly to go about our business. As it turned out, we weren't really in danger and nothing happened.

We were given cigarette and beer rations in Corsica. I didn't use either at that time, so I traded my cigarettes and beer for candy. Not that I had that much of a sweet tooth, but a woman living maybe two miles from the airbase had a laundry business. I didn't want to do my own laundry, so I gave her candy and she did it for me. I watched her and a few other ladies washing clothes one day. They'd go down to a beautiful stream and work the heck out of the clothes in the water. They'd beat the clothes on rocks and then spread them out to dry. They spent untold hours doing a single load of laundry. But when I got my clothes back, they were clean. It was really neat.

The B-25 was a formidable flying machine. There were twin .50 caliber machineguns in the tail, on each side, on the top, and the pilot had control of forward firing twin .50s on either side of the fuselage. The plane had withering firepower. As the bombardier/navigator, I rode in a Plexiglas dome in the nose of the plane where I had a .50 caliber machinegun that I could fire through the nose.

Not long after we got to Corsica, we took off on a mission, heading north. A plane that I couldn't identify flew directly at us. Our pilot had alerted others on the crew. It came out of the north, straight at us, and in line with some hills behind it. Thus, I couldn't distinguish what it was. I got on my machinegun but didn't fire. Luckily, none of us fired because it turned out to be a friendly P-47. If the plane had been an enemy and we had waited until he fired, it could have been too late for us.

In some of the seminars we attended back in the States, we were trained in aircraft recognition. A special projector, called a tachistoscope, would flash the image of a plane onto a screen for a very brief period of time. As we got better and better at identifying planes, the times got shorter and shorter, as short as $1/100^{th}$ of a second. The strangest thing is we could do it!

The Corsican countryside was absolutely beautiful. I've used that word a number of times, but I don't know how better to explain what I saw. Corsica is very mountainous so most of the population is situated on or near the coast, but even the cities and towns there are spread out because of the terrain. Across the mountains west from Ghisonaccia is Ajaccio, the capital and largest city, also where Napoleon was born.

There were three of us who decided one day that we wanted to swim. The small river nearby was too shallow, the same stream in which the ladies washed clothes. We decided we'd follow the river upstream to see if we could find a place that was a little deeper. We rounded several bends in the streambed, but we weren't finding anything and were about to give up. One of the fellows said, "Let's go around this next bend."

We went around the next bend and, honest to Pete, there was the most inviting thing you could imagine. There was a huge rock, maybe 10 feet tall, with the stream flowing down on each side. Below lay a solid rock formation, but over the eons, the water flow had carved out what amounted to a big bowl. The center of this bowl had to be at least 10 feet deep. On each side of the stream were niches carved out of the rock, level places on which to lie and where the sun would hit at certain times of the day. We used those niches for tanning beds, diving platforms, and as great places to relax.

The water flowed down from the mountains absolutely ice-cold. It was wonderful, the most exhilarating thing ever, especially after dealing with the heat. When I saw the pool and surrounding rocks, it reminded me to a minor degree of the Vesuvius Pool at Coral Gables. It was magnificent. We spent a lot of our off-duty time there.

As I swam one day, I noticed that there was an eel in the pool with me. I wasn't too sure I liked that arrangement, but he didn't bother me and I certainly didn't bother him. Another day, as I sunned myself on one of the ledges, I glanced down to the bottom of the pool and saw an object. I dove down and got it, a Boy Scout knife. I kept that knife for years after returning to civilian life, but eventually lost track of it. I don't know what happened to it.

One day a group of us walked from the base up toward the swimming hole. As we rounded a curve in the riverbed, I had a sudden dizzy sensation. The land in front of me was moving! That was just an illusion caused by countless turtles on the banks of the river. The bank I'm describing was a flat area about 15x25 feet in area, and the whole thing seemed to be moving. On average, most of the turtles were probably eight inches across the shell, about the same size as the rocks in the area. Thus, at first glance it looked like the rocks were moving. That's what caused the optical illusion, making me think the ground was moving.

We didn't walk through the turtles—we gave them ample berth and walked around them to get to the pool.

The size of the turtles amazed me and to see so many of them at one time. I'm sure that a lot of them wound up in soup. The natives probably had a number of turtle recipes. With the shortage of food in Corsica, one of the things that surprised me was that, here was this plentiful supply and I wondered why it still existed. Why hadn't the natives decimated the turtles for food? I'm sure the indigenous people would have been more than willing to eat the turtles. I've had turtle soup but never just turtle meat. As a kid, I've had turtles that I caught and then carried them in a burlap bag, only to have them spoil. That was a disgusting sight and smell.

I've told this story to quite a few outdoorsmen who know something about marine and reptile life, but no one has told me what all those turtles were doing there. I'd like to find out what caused their movement. I'm aware of the mass migration of baby turtles toward the sea when they hatch, but these weren't babies. Where did all these large turtles come from and where were they going? Those are questions that haven't been answered for me yet.

While we were in Corsica, a B-24 got hit during a combat run and had to land at our base. They had probably been bombing some industrial area in France. Their base was in Italy but their plane had some serious engine problems, forcing them down for repairs.

Among the crew members of the B-24 was a piano player, a lieutenant. We had a piano in our rec room and he'd play for us while he was there. He played by ear, almost any kind of music but mostly popular stuff. He played New Orleans-style blues and bebop before bebop had really become known. He'd just hammer the heck out of our piano. We really enjoyed having him there. He really was good. We arranged with the mechanics on base to delay repair of the lieutenant's plane so that we could hear him play some more. We kept him as long as we could, until we finally got a direct order from LTG Wall to get that plane repaired and back to Italy!

On the base we had latrines that were set up and properly maintained. But as far as personal sanitation was concerned, there were no real showers or baths. That's the major reason we went looking for a swimming pool. We just didn't have anything else. Otherwise, we had to take a bath using our helmets to hold the bathwater.

One night, it was late and I had put some water in my helmet for me to wash with in the morning. I set it near my cot by the windowsill. Later that night, I woke up and heard something messing around in the water. A rat had gotten into my helmet. I wasn't about to mess with the rat, but I managed to cover the helmet and kept him in there until he drowned.

The next day, we were in the mess hall and I told some of the men about the rat. They told me that there were rats all over the island. Luckily, that was the only one we ever found in our quarters.

A few days later, several of us were talking at a table after lunch when one of the fellows said, "Gee, look at that."

We saw a rat running on a wire from our building to the one next door. The agility of those animals was amazing, how they could get up on a little tiny wire and actually scamper along on it. We just watched him—didn't try to get him.

There was a special person I remember from my original crew, our radio/gunner. He was a young fellow, a Jewish boy from New York City, named Bernie Plotkin. He was just happy, go-lucky, a nice young man to be around, full of excitement and enthusiasm.

While we were in Homestead on our way overseas, Bernie and I went into the PX (Post Exchange, a military department store) to pick up some last-minute supplies. One of the salesgirls there wore a sweater and on the left front she wore a tag that said "Betty."

Bernie looked at her and asked, "Do you mind if I ask you a question?" She said that would be okay, so he asked her, "What do you call the other one?"

Betty didn't think that was the least bit funny but I never forgot it. Bernie could liven up any get-together.

While we were in Corsica, Bernie got word that his wife and infant son had been hit by an out-of-control truck on a New York City street. Both of them died from their injuries. From there on, Bernie just went into his shell. When I heard about it, I tried to console him but he wouldn't even speak. He couldn't. I've got a letter that he wrote later that explained what he felt at the time.

Gosh, such bright spots in his life, and then to all of a sudden have that calamity happen, him not being anywhere near his family or be able to do anything about it. War is hell in a lot of different ways. Physical injuries take their toll but mental anguish, though unseen, can wreak havoc if untreated.

5.
COMBAT

I kept a diary back at home base (Appendix A), which I updated after each combat mission. In it I recorded such things as target, target location, length of mission, and bombs carried. Of the latter, a typical entry might read "4x1000," indicating we were carrying four bombs, a thousand-pound each. Some of the entries in the diary have a "XX," indicating that we were on a practice run or weren't able to release our bomb load due to weather or some other problem.

Regarding the time of flight for each mission listed in the diary, figure about 250 miles an hour or a little faster as the average speed to calculate the distance to and from the target. The times listed are from wheels up to wheels down, in other words the complete mission from beginning to end. The plane would be going about 300 mph approaching the target. Once the bombs were released, the plane would turn and drop, picking up speed in order to make a quick escape.

I probably shouldn't have kept a diary, but I did. We were told that the Germans would have been very interested in it had they ever captured our base. What follows is an elaborated version of those events:

June 2, 1944
Our first mission was to bomb the bridges and viaducts at Borgo San Lorenzo, which we did successfully.

The pilot got us set on our bombing runs. He'd fly to what we called the IP, or initial point. That's where the bombardier took over flying the plane. The Norden bombsight was electrically linked to the flight controls. When the pilot turned the plane over to the bombardier, he'd have it headed on the right course toward the target.

My job as bombardier was this: The course line was a straight line, our heading, and had to be put on the target and centered there. I had to compensate for any drift by tweaking the dials on the bombsight. With the airspeed and everything else calculated correctly, the rate line would hold steady with the crosshairs locked on the target. The bomb sight automatically did its computing and, when its internal workings matched the cross hairs, bombs from the airplane were released automatically. As soon as the bombs dropped, I'd close the bomb bay doors and yell, "Bombs away!" to tell the pilot that the plane was back in his control. We really wouldn't have had to tell our pilots that but we always did.

The instant the bombs were away, we were away. We'd come off the target probably doing over 400 mph, straining everything in the airplane, but we wanted to get out of there really fast.

On this, our first mission, we didn't encounter any flak—a peaceful flight all the way through. One thing that we had to watch for over Italy, in flying over the mountains we had to be careful because there were tracers that the Germans fired from the ground. They had a limited range, but on one occasion we had just come off our target and by relative standards we were flying pretty low. As we passed between two mountain peaks, we received tracer fire from the peak on our left. Our plane got hit and one of the rounds clipped the throat mike on our radio-gunner. The bullet didn't touch him, didn't even leave a red mark. The bullet just tore the microphone off his neck and continued out through the fuselage on the other side of the airplane.

Tracers are just ordinary bullets, but with a chemical coating that makes them glow in flight. The thing about tracers is that, between tracers, there may be anywhere from four up to eight or 10 other bullets. The tracers gave the gunner ranging capability so he knew exactly where all of his bullets are going, and scared the hell out of us who were targets.

June 4
Two days later, we went after a railroad bridge NW of Pesaro on the northeast coast of Italy, but missed the target. We did peripheral damage to the railroad tracks but didn't take out the bridge, our bombs falling wide. The lead bombardier had to have been off on his course. We went back later and took out that bridge. Missing our target didn't happen very often.

Very often, even though the bomb drop didn't center on the target properly, the little variation in bomb spacing between the lead plane and the outside plane could result in a bulls-eye. The lead bombardier might inflict peripheral damage while one of the planes at the side of the echelon would nail the main target. Even if that didn't happen, the peripheral damage could be significant, fully justifying the mission.

June 5

We were assigned a nickeling mission at Terni, just north of Rome, "nickels" being propaganda sheets or leaflets printed in the local language of France, Italy, or whatever was appropriate. The nickels encouraged civilians on the ground to help the Allies, do what they could to disrupt or impede the Germans, or at least not do anything to help the enemy. My 30 missions (actually 29 2/3!) included several nickeling missions.

Our bombing missions took place at altitudes between eight and 12 thousand feet, and our nickeling missions at altitudes between six and eight thousand feet.

On this mission, we flew over Italy near Mount Etna, an active volcano. You may recall Etna erupting during WWII. When the eruption occurred, there were a number B-17s in the area that got loaded down with a very heavy layer of volcanic ash on their wings. Some of the planes were damaged by the weight of the ash. On the sides of the mountain, we could see the results of previous eruptions. There were remains of structures sticking up through the lava—interesting to see, but eerie.

As we flew to Terni, the weather closed in and we couldn't see the drop area for our nickels. So we circled back and landed at Vesuviano, by then in Allied control, where we spent the night. We stayed in a two-story brick building, one of two that were part of a slum clearance or urban renewal project directed by Mussolini a few years earlier. Those two brick buildings were parallel, each probably 200 feet long and 100 yards apart. Our building had a hallway down the middle and rooms on each side. We were in one building and there were local civilians in the other.

Near one end of our building stood the mess hall and outside it were garbage disposal drums. We were in our quarters, upstairs just standing there idly looking out of the window. We had just finished supper and the KPs were finishing cleanup, including dumping garbage in the drums outside the mess hall.

When the KPs were finished, civilians came out of the other building, many of them carrying containers. They went to the disposal drums, opened them, and practically dove in, reaching up to their shoulders to get at the food scraps inside. For a long time thereafter, for years in fact, I just couldn't leave anything on my plate. Even today, I think of that incident whenever I can't finish a meal.

The slum clearance had been good for those civilians. They'd been moved out of the hovels they'd been in and moved into the new, brick building. They had a nice place to stay but little food. The Italian people went through hell. Between the war and some of the other things Mussolini had done, the civilians were in dire straits.

AT A TWELFTH AIR FORCE B-25 BASE... Flak ? Oh yes - flak !

Second Lieutenant Erwin E. Carmen has seen plenty of it.

He is a bombardier-navigator on a B-25 with a Twelfth Air Force B-25 Mitchell medium bomber group.

His advanced navigation training was received at Coral Gables, Florida, and his bombing training at Carlsbad, New Mexico. He was sent to Greeneville, South Carolina for further combat training.

Since his coming to this theater, nine missions have been flown by Lieutenant Carmen.

"Flak ?" he asks, "Oh yes, flak ! I've seen some of it - too much of it already. And me only a rookie ! "

He continues: "No known flak, that is their reason for choosing the way we are to enter the target area. But it so happens, after some decided setbacks, Jerry has concentrated more guns around our very target.

"We hit the I.P. and start on the bomb run. One minute everything's rosy, then the sky begins to act very queerly.

"Those are'nt just black spots in front of my eyes !

"The realization that flak is bursting awfully damned close breaks into the fascinated cells that should be my brain. I watch four gun bursts ahead and high, then suddenly a burst at 12 o'clock on altitude.

"I await in fearful watchfulness, because I know the next burst or the third will get us. I crawl into myself like a turtle and wait".

MORE

Air Corps Press Release

"But the burst does'nt come !

"I wipe my brow and thank God that my introduction was to a single gun and not the four gun battery to our right".

Lieutenant Carman is the son of Mrs. Esther D. Volz, Route 3, Saginaw, Michigan.

Having graduated from the Northern High School, Flint, Michigan in June, 1936, he held a position as follow-up man in the parts distribution office of the Chevrolet Motor Company.

Commanding Lieutenant Carman's squadron is Major L. Hill of Foley, Alabama.

Lt. Carman's wife, Elsie, and their four year old son reside at 1019 north Stevenson Street in Flint.

Air Corps Press Release (continued)

Miscellaneous:

Pfc. Ralph W. Harwick, whose wife, Ruth, lives at 707 Prospect St., is a member of a flight test crew at an Air Service Command depot in England.

Pvt. Raymond Leopold MacArthur, whose wife, Helen, and children live at 615 Leland St., son of Mr. and Mrs. Alex MacArthur, 910 Avon St., is attending a specialist course in communications at Camp Davis, N. C.

Pfc. William H. Ostrom, son of William Ostrom, 1632 Arizona Ave., has informed his father and relatives that he was stung by a Portugese man-of-war fish while swimming off the coast of New Guinea recently.

1st Lt. George Yaskanin, son of Mr. and Mrs. Peter Yaskanin, Linden, is serving overseas as signal supply and maintenance officer at a service command station somewhere in the ETO.

Lt. Carman

2nd Lt. Erwin E. Carman, whose wife, Elsie, and son, live at 1019 N. Stevenson St., son of Mrs. Esther D. Volz, Saginaw, is a bombardier - navigator of a B-25 with the 12th Air Force B-25 Mitchel medium bomber group, in Corsica.

Reg., IRTC, Camp Blanding, Fla.

Pvt. Everette L. Warner, son of Mr. and Mrs. Lloyd Warner, Otisville, ASN 36522809, Co. B, 18th Bn., 5th Reg., APO 411, Fort George G. Meade, Md.

Dale D. Princing, S2c, whose wife, Lois, and children live at 1254 W. Juliah Ave., son of Mr. and Mrs. Delbert Princing, 1085 Yale Ave., Ship Receiving Div., 4, Terminal Island, San Pedro, Calif.

Cpl. Robert W. Goodall, son of Mr. and Mrs. William L. Goodall, 2518 N. Saginaw St., ASN 3658-1822, APO 322, c/o Postmaster, San Francisco, Calif.

Pfc. Huberties A. Plant, Jr., son of Mr. and Mrs. Huberties Plant, Elberta, formerly of Flint, ASN 16063344, APO 519, c/o Postmaster, New York City.

Walter C. Hayes, S2c, whose wife, Joyce, lives at 8235 Corunna Rd., Unit 2, 12th Bn., Brks. 1244, Shoemaker, Calif.

Kenneth E. Morse, HA1c, son of Mrs. Olga Morse, 1713 Oak St., Med. Det., Camp Lejeune, N. C.

Gerald (Jerry) Mesack, S1c, son of Mrs. W. A. Sobey, Swartz Creek, General Delivery, Bldg. 4102, USNTS, Newport, R. I.

Kenneth W. Woodfield, F2c, son of Mr. and Mrs. Walter Woodfield, 1414 Smith St., Co. 1144, OGU, Great Lakes, Ill.

A/C Edward H. Viall, son of Mr. and Mrs. Edward J. Viall, 315 W. Rankin St., ASN 3687-

Flint Journal, Sunday, July 16, 1944

June 6

We left Vesuviano, dropped our nickels on Terni, and returned to our base. We flew more similar missions, which proved to be easy ones with no particular excitement.

We were airborne and on the way to our target when we learned of the D-Day invasion. We had just crossed the west coast of Italy when we heard the news. Everybody cheered, knowing that the war would be ending soon.

There was an encampment of German soldiers, a regiment, near Terni. By the time we were shot down two months later, the Allies had taken that area and, in fact, had moved way up north in Italy. On our way back to base that day, we saw nine bursts of flak over Stimigliano. Luckily, it was far enough away that we didn't sustain any damage. We were always relieved to see the flak because it told us how good the gunners on the ground were—far away flak meant the gunnery was not too accurate.

There were some missions where we didn't encounter flak. Those were the kind we liked! Our flak encounters weren't just during bombing missions. We ran into it during nickeling missions, too, because those flights were over enemy territory. We had quite a bit of feedback from the nickeling missions, informing us what the Germans were doing.

June 6 was our third consecutive day flying a mission, but then we skipped a few days. The flight crews needed some time out, but our planes also needed work. We had down time but the mechanics were busy performing maintenance and repairs on our aircraft. On each return flight, even if we hadn't been hit, the ground crew went over the plane with a fine-tooth comb. They were really good, fast, and efficient. If a plane came in damaged one day, unless it was badly damaged, it would be ready for a mission the next day.

June 9

We returned to Pesaro, Italy, and destroyed a railroad bridge that we had missed a few days earlier. Going back to Pesaro was good—we made up for the previous miss— but we were coming on-target at the same altitude and speed, and the gunners on the ground could use that to their advantage. Fortunately, the flak was light.

It's hard to explain a miss; it truly is. We had not only the lead plane and its bombs, we had the other planes in the lead echelon and the planes in the trailing echelons, all releasing bombs over the target. There was always peripheral damage inflicted, but this time that damage was minor. Most importantly, we somehow missed our mark. On this, our second go-around, we got the main target.

June 10

We destroyed railroad bridges northwest of Montenero, Italy. Our bombing pattern on those objectives was just excellent—we couldn't have done any better if we had been on the ground and placed the bombs manually at the targets.

We encountered heavy flak. The gunners on the ground, the Germans, didn't wait for our aircraft to reach the IP before they began firing. They were firing as soon as they saw us and we were in range. Many times our target would be completely covered with flak before we ever got to the IP. That made for interesting flying, and that's what we ran into over Montenero. Our plane got hit by pieces of shrapnel (bomb pieces) but nobody was hurt. As badly damaged as our plane was, it's a miracle no one was injured.

The Germans were pretty darn good with their ack-ack (anti-aircraft fire). They had 85mm and 105mm guns that were deadly, and they knew how to use them. Up until that time, I hadn't considered the danger we were in. When the flak started flying, for some reason I hadn't been concerned and suspect the other members of the crew felt the same way. But when I saw that first plane go down I said, *Hmm, it* could *happen to me.* That changed my thinking and brought me back to reality.

I don't remember any of the crew ever expressing any kind of complaint or essence of fear whenever the flak started flying. They did nothing of the sort, not even after that initial wake-up call. We were all too focused on our mission.

June 14

We destroyed a railroad tunnel east of Prato, Italy.

The Germans had antiaircraft guns mounted on trucks and even on railroad cars. Of course, with one mounted on a railroad car, there are only certain places they could go— they needed tracks. The point being, they could move those guns around at will. They had a shortage of armament so they had to move it to wherever they thought it needed to be.

Italy is a scenic country, especially when viewed from 8000 feet in the air. But those rolling hills so often held gun emplacements manned by people trying to knock us down. The flight to Prato was both pleasurable and anxiety-inducing. We encountered less flak than we had expected.

June 15
We destroyed a railroad bridge and marshalling yards at Viareggio, Italy.

Viareggio is just north of Pisa on the west coast of Italy. The Leaning Tower of Pisa was easily visible to us. On this run, we were thankful for light flak in the target area.

June 16
We destroyed a railroad bridge south of Vernio, Italy. Our bombs had good concentration. We received heavy flak.

When I say we had "good concentration," I mean that everybody hit their targets. When the bombs were dropped, the natural inclination for most bombardiers was to kind of relax and get away from the bombsight. But my inclination was to get up further into the Plexiglas nose so I could see what was happening below. I wanted to see where those bombs hit on the ground.

For some reason or another, the Germans guarded that bridge heavily, making our mission to Vernio a tough one. We had quite a few planes hit, including ours, but none went down. Our plane had shrapnel in both wings and the rudder, but nothing in the cabin. I can still close my eyes and see walls of flak.

En route to the IP, the pilot had to keep the plane on course to the target. Once at the IP, the lead bombardier took control of the plane through his Norden bombsight, but until then the pilot had to knowingly guide the plane, sometimes through a wall of flak. Meanwhile, I could focus on looking at the target through my bombsight and let the pilot worry about the anti-aircraft fire. I tried to not even think about the explosions taking place nearby. We had a mission to perform and couldn't consider anything else.

June 17

We tried to bomb heavy gun emplacements on the island of Elba, but weather forced our return to base.

We're talking about the town of Elba, in Italy, not the island where Napoleon had been exiled. We encountered towering cumulus clouds, tall and black, so we returned to base without dropping our bombs. This was close to home and we really wanted to take out those guns. Heavy cloud cover obscured the target. Other American forces later took Elba.

All aircraft follow the same set of rules, whereby planes fly at different assigned altitudes to avoid midair collisions. If you're flying in one direction, you fly at a certain altitude or multiple thereof; if you're flying in a different direction, you fly at a different altitude or multiple thereof.

That morning, we had just taken off and were rising to our assigned altitude when another plane came in for a landing. We had hit the impasse point. Fortunately, it was a friendly plane. Our pilot and their pilot each took corrective action and we avoided disaster.

To us, it was a scary situation because we were still new to the game. We were sure there was a German, a German pilot, or a bombardment coming at us from every direction. Whenever we'd see an airplane we couldn't identify right away or somewhere we didn't expect it to be, we got skittish.

June 21
We flew to Vistoia, Italy, where there was a viaduct that needed to come out. We hit the target hard—our bomb concentration was excellent. There was no question that the viaduct was out of commission when we left. But we saw the most intense flak ever over the town of Pisticci. You could almost walk on it; it really was heavy.

On that flight, for whatever reason, our bomb bay doors stuck open and stayed open all the way back to home base. As a result, loose papers, maps, and other items got sucked out of the plane. That made for an interesting flight.

June 22
We hit an SAP target north of Vernio, Italy, and ran into heavy flak again. We had 11 ships lost or damaged. SAP means we used Semi-Armor Piercing munitions.

Vernio could have outpaced Ferarra as far as flak intensity and accuracy was concerned. We were after a railroad bridge and marshalling yards. Along with our squadron, nearby flew a B-26 group out of Bastia, on the northern tip of Corsica, heading in the same direction but after targets further north. They got the hell shot out of them and I saw two of them go down. One plane got hit and we saw at least some of the crew parachute from it. The second plane got hit hard; its wings wavered before it rolled over and nosed on down, streaming black smoke. It never straightened up and we saw no parachutes ejecting, so we had to presume that all of the crew died.

That was the first time I saw Allied planes get shot down and it brought me to a stark reality: Those planes had been downed by antiaircraft fire! That was a surreal experience. As I watched the planes go down, I kept thinking, *This isn't happening; it's just a movie.*

It was almost a blessing when we saw flak bursting because then we knew where it was. That relieved the anxiety; at least it did when the bursts were far away because we knew we weren't in immediate danger.

On this particular mission, the sky was black with flak. I don't know where all the German guns came from, but they had to have a mess of them on the ground. The pilots were flying into this stuff. Just before the two B-26s went down, it seemed as though the flak had deepened a shade or two.

We had12 planes in our squadron, four echelons of three each, but there was also a squadron of B-26s involved, so not all the losses were from our squadron. In fact, the B-26s sustained the most losses. I saw at least two planes go down and several others got hit. I couldn't tell you how many were damaged all together.

It just dawned on me that I seldom saw just one plane go down—they always seemed to go down in pairs. Fortunately, I never saw more than two planes go down on a single mission, but rarely just one.

We didn't lose a plane in our squadron, although several were hit.

June 25

We flew a practice mission, but weather forced us to abort the bombing run and return to base. "We" in this case was just our crew and plane. One of the objectives was to check out my dual navigator/bombardier ratings for future assignments.

The "XX" in my log indicates no targets were acquired. In this case, it was just a practice bombing run so that notation would have been entered even if the weather hadn't forced the mission to be aborted. I used the same notation whenever we were on a mission that we had to abort without dropping our bombs.

June 29

We destroyed a rail and highway bridge at Pietra Ligure, Italy, near the French border. It turned out to be another of those welcome runs. No flak! None!

We were anxious to get into France, knowing that it would mean the Allies were moving north and the war would soon be over. This day we came within 20 miles. Our bombing missions were intended to disrupt German transportation, making it harder for them to resist the Allied advance. I don't recall bombing any highways or roadways, at least not as specific targets. We were after railway bridges and other railway elements, such as viaducts and marshalling yards. We took out a highway or highway bridge only if it happened to cross our railroad objective.

June 30
We made a direct hit on a rail viaduct south of Marradi, Italy, and inflicted significant peripheral damage. We encountered no flak on this mission.

COL Ward came along as an observer on this mission and he commented, "A cake walk!" He was our wing commander and rarely flew with us. Our group had been given a presidential citation for having flown more missions than any other group in the area and COL Ward came along as a way of patting us on the back, encouraging us to fly some more!

July 1
We inflicted only minor damage on a fuel dump at Marina di Ravenna because some of our bombs hung up. We encountered light and inaccurate flak.

There must have been some sort of miscalculation by the lead bombardier because we missed our primary target badly. We didn't make enough hits on the target to warrant the mission. I just can't tell you what a sinking feeling that was. The bombs were away but we could see they were way off target. There was nothing more we could do, except go back to home base. The lead bombardier held his head down for a while.

The reason we used 100-pound bombs on this mission, instead of something heavier, is that they were a fragmentation munitions. When they went off, they sent shrapnel all over the place. When we were after a fuel dump, we wanted to rupture as many tanks as possible. Unfortunately, we didn't do too well that day, didn't ruin as many tanks as we had hoped.

July 6
We were directed to bomb the construction headquarters of a German outfit called TODT, a German construction outfit named after its founder, Fritz Todt, an engineer and a senior Nazi.

The TODT mission was to repair all the targets we had bombed. That HQ had all kinds of heavy construction equipment used to repair the bridges and viaducts. The Germans had a defense line set up near Florence that TODT had been instrumental in building. I think we overran them. They were in the midst of trying to get things done and we got there too soon for them.

We flew over Terme on the way to the target and on the way back to base, encountering flak and tracers both times. We completely destroyed the target, but ran into tracers. That scared the fool out of me, because every time I saw a red line, I knew there are several other bullets in between that and the next red line. The red lines were very close together.

We saw tracers as we approached the target, we saw tracers as we were leaving the target, there were tracers coming at us fulltime. That was unnerving. The closer the tracers, the more unnerving it became, but fortunately we were out of their range. Those guns were probably in the neighborhood of .50 calibers, not capable our reaching our altitude. I really don't understand why they were even firing.

July 8

We missed a railway bridge southwest of Ferrara, Italy, a heavily defended site. We missed the bridge but hit marshalling yards north of target. We received heavy flak but suffered no hits on our plane.

That was one instance where the peripheral damage was nearly as good as a direct hit. We were supposed to take out the bridge that served the marshalling yards, but we took out the marshalling yards instead, which amounted to about the same thing. The bridge was useless so that worked out pretty well.

The Corps had a scoring system and when you reached 75 points you were rotated back home. I say "the Corps," but it may have been each group or squadron commander who set up his own scoring system, probably the group commander. I don't recall now exactly how the scoring system worked, what had to be done to get points, but it was something like so many points per mission.

By the time I realized they even had a point system, I was within about 20 points of the 75 needed. I wanted to up the ante and get to 75 faster, so I volunteered on a number of occasions to fly with other crews. My crew typically flew a mission one day and then was off the next, but by volunteering I could fly practically every day. If another crew needed a bombardier/navigator, I could fly with them for extra points.

On one of the missions for which I volunteered, Hal Moore recommended me as the navigator/bombardier. During that mission, we had an observer with us—I don't recall his rank—and he got hit with flak. I could see just a small puncture wound but he bled to death during our flight back to Corsica. I remember him standing by the gun turret when he got hit, the one on top of our plane. He knew immediately that he'd been hit but had no idea that it was serious. He was lucid and talking just fine. We were talking to each other, but by the time we got home he was pretty weak and by the time they got him to the hospital he was dead. The shrapnel must have destroyed major organs or arteries, making a seemingly minor wound fatal.

July 10

We flew to Cremona, Italy, and took out the marshalling yards there without encountering any flak. We expected flak but didn't get it, a welcome occurrence after what we had experienced at Ferrara.

This was one of my volunteer missions, flying with LT Brett and his crew.

July 11

On a mission to Alessandra, Italy, we took out another railroad marshalling yard and there just happened to be an engine on-site, along with an immense number of freight cars. The engine we hit wasn't moving, just sitting there and, by golly, we got it!

That was the first engine we'd seen on any of our missions. The Germans were obviously planning a massive movement to account for all the rolling stock there. We should have been patted on the back for that one, but weren't.

We also hit a nearby munitions plant, another big bonus. On that mission we encountered no ack-ack. We liked those "milk runs" where we didn't see any flak.

July 12

On this particular day, we were after a railway bridge near Borgoforte, Italy. We scored direct hits on our objective anyway in an amusing way.

The Germans used smoke pots, setting them on the bridge to obscure our target. But the wind came up, blowing the smoke away from the target. The result, as seen from the air, was like a big arrow pointing directly at the bridge. We just followed the arrow and then released our bombs. We appreciated the help! But we really did use our bombsights, too.

As we were coming back to base from Borgoforte, we were in our landing pattern and headed for touchdown when part of the Plexiglas nose of the airplane disintegrated right in front of me. I thought, *My God, I'm hit!*

A week or so before that, some of the aerial gunners on our base were doing tracking exercises when one of them accidentally pulled his trigger, spraying errant live rounds. No one got hurt, but it made us all aware that there were shooters on the ground. So, when the nose of my airplane caved in, the first thing I thought of were those aerial gunners and figured there'd been another accident. I had blood all over me. And feathers—we had hit a large bird! None of the blood was mine, fortunately.

Later, the crew awarded me a huge purple heart with feathers on it. They harassed me about that incident for the longest time.

July 13

Our squadron, one echelon composed of three airplanes, destroyed a pontoon bridge on the Po River near San Nicola, Italy. We made one direct hit on the south approach to the bridge.

Again, we encountered no flak.

We returned to base and learned that a second mission awaited us that day: We were to bomb a railroad bridge near Borgoforte, but towering clouds over the area forced us to return to base without dropping our bombs.

July 14

We tried to bomb a pontoon bridge at Polesella, Italy, but again heavy overcast forced us to return to base without dropping our bombs.

We often wondered about some of the targets that higher headquarters picked out for us. But a pontoon bridge was very effective and could carry a heavy load. The Germans could run trucks, tanks, anything across it. The pontoon bridges may have been a little wobbly when heavier loads crossed it, but they worked. We didn't question our targets or the thinking behind them; we just went and got them.

Returning to base with all our bombs was something we didn't like to do. So many things could happen. The bombs hung on suspension units in the bomb bay. They were electronically controlled and those controls could fail. When we loaded the bombs into the airplane, as the bombardier I was the guy who pulled the pins that activated or armed the bombs. When we returned from a mission without dropping our load, I had to replace the pins in all the bombs to deactivate them. We always appreciated smooth landings, especially with a load of live bombs!

July 15
We destroyed a pontoon bridge at Ficarolo, Italy, encountering inaccurate flak once on the way to target and three times on our return. Our run also resulted in blockage of an adjacent highway. Fortunately, none of the flak was very accurate.

July 16
We did a run on a railroad bridge in Materna, Italy, and hit the target very effectively. We encountered only light flak, but we caught some of it on the tail of our airplane. Both rudders had damage but, fortunately, the tail-gunner was unharmed. We could never tell what was going to happen.

When we got back from the flight, I went to the mechanics and told them, "I want an iron plate put under my seat in the nose of the plane."

So, under the seat cushion they fixed an iron plate so that if shrapnel came up through the bottom of the plane it'd have to go through that plate first and might not get to me. I didn't want any of that stuff hitting my butt.

July 19

We were on our way to bomb a highway bridge near Ferrara, Italy, and that day we could have walked on the flak. It was so heavy and accurate. It's just a wonder that any airplane made it through it. Many of our planes were hit but not hard enough to lose any. Our squadron came through alright, no injuries, but I couldn't verify that for the other squadrons involved.

It wasn't unusual to return from a mission with holes in our airplanes. What was unusual was that most of those bursts didn't hit people. On that particular occasion, we got to within 15 minutes of the target and the weather was so bad that we had to cancel the mission. Thank Heaven! The bridge was very heavily defended. We learned later that a B-26 group that preceded us in the target area caught hell—no specifics were given.

July 20

The day after that "thank Heaven" flight, we went back to Ferrara. That time we hit it lucky because we ran into very little flak and we got the bridge without any problems.

This was another mission where we saw a squadron of B-26s out of Bastia headed in the same general direction as us, but after different targets. Their group flew ahead of us and hit their targets before we hit ours. We were both after targets in a similar geographical area. On this occasion, I was happy they were ahead of us and drawing all the ground fire. Also, they were after more heavily-defended targets further north. The B-26s always seemed to draw heavier fire, while we were relatively unscathed—not that I complained.

When we later got into France, that's when we started to see the air defense pick up substantially, and for good reason. Our air attacks were closing in on the German homeland.

In a way, it's amusing that we'd bomb bridges and then later rebuild them so that the Allies could use them.

July 23

On a third strike on Ferrara, we ran into heavy flak again. Adding insult to injury, we missed our target, at least that's the way it looked to me as I watched through the Plexiglas nose of our plane.

Usually, just one plane in a formation would have camera equipment to document what went on during a bombing mission. Some of the earlier photos showed little or no damage, but later photos showed significant damage to the target. Thus, we were vindicated.

Designated airplanes had cameras aboard. When we released our bombs, we took off and were gone as quickly as possible. However, other airplanes would be flying behind us and had not yet come off the target. In this case, photos taken by a plane in a later echelon saw damage inflicted that our camera hadn't picked up. Apparently a plane in one of the echelons behind us nailed the target we had missed. We didn't hit the bulls-eye but one of our sister planes did.

Also, there were two squadrons involved with each having a lead bombardier. The lead bombardier in my squadron missed the target, but the lead bombardier in the second squadron nailed it. That's where the discrepancy comes in, regarding the pictures taken by the plane in our squadron.

The Germans sent up a ton of ack-ack and we received a direct hit. Fortunately, the shell that hit us didn't have a proximity fuse or it would have blown us out of the sky. Rather, it had been set to blow up at a higher altitude, so it went through the plane and exploded above us.

We felt the plane shudder when the shell hit. I called all the stations to see if everyone was alright, but the tail-gunner didn't answer. I crawled over the bomb bay and headed toward the rear of the plane. The tail-gunner's name was P.A. Reed—I called him Prince Albert. When I got back there, I found him slumped over his guns. When I reached out to touch him on the shoulder, his arm came off in my hand. He never knew what hit him, never even knew he'd been hit.

Again, there were some Allied B-26s flying out of Bastia where they were based. We were bound for a target north of Florence, Italy, and they were on a mission a little deeper into the country. They caught hell. Our squadrons were in sight of each other and we could even see their target way off in the distance. We saw two planes go down—the flak was just terrible where they were. They were catching all kinds of fire.

July 24

We went to P.A. Reed's funeral and interment at Bastia, where there was a large military cemetery. Three other officers rode with me in one jeep: our commanding officer, MAJ Hill; LT Gimson, the pilot of the plane on which Reed had flown; LT Moore; and me. The rest of LT Gimson's crew rode in another jeep.

That was a bittersweet experience because the occasion was so solemn, but the scenery en route was so beautiful. Bastia itself is an amazing sight. We never got the chance to spend time there, just drove to the cemetery and back to our base.

In every old picture of a European town or village, houses seem to be built almost touching and stair-stepping up a steep grade. That's the way Bastia was, a very pretty town. The old homes there were built on the foothills and were wall-to-wall—a view from the past that survives today. We saw it from a different angle on several missions that took us over the city.

July 27

Our mission was to bomb a railroad bridge at Borgoforte, but we had to drop out of formation and return to base because of engine trouble with our plane. The rest of the squadron continued on and completed the mission. We felt a big let-down, having been all eager and ready to go, only to have to limp back to base.

One of the pilots in our squadron had flown quite a few missions, enough that he should have been sent home. He was a cocky, know-it-all, brash individual. One day, while taxiing out to the take-off point, he tried to get as close as possible to the next airplane. He clipped the wing of a neighboring aircraft. He didn't do damage to the other plane but he damaged the wing of his own. That was sufficient in his own mind to abort the mission, so we didn't even get off the ground.

The ground crew called for an immediate inspection of both planes. Minor damage to a plane can make a major difference in its flight characteristics. The inspector signaled for the other plane to take off, but thumbed us out. Our pilot was delighted—he thought that was great—he didn't want to go anyway.

We had to watch him very carefully. Finally, he got relieved of duty and sent to a hospital. We didn't have post traumatic stress syndrome in those days. Well, we did and some folks suffered from it, but the condition hadn't been officially identified.

July 29

We couldn't see our target, a railroad bridge at Ferrara, because of weather.

We flew south, away from the weather formation, and crossed the Italian peninsula and over the Adriatic. There we flew north again, hoping to come in from the other side. But the cloud cover over the target was just as heavy from that side, too. Trying to approach Ferrara from another direction didn't work either, so we had to abort the mission and return to base.

Ferrara is not far off the Adriatic coast in northeastern Italy. There were German ships in the Adriatic but they didn't necessarily bother us at the altitudes we were flying. Flying over land was much more dangerous as that's where the Germans had most of their ack-ack artillery. The Germans still occupied parts of northern Italy, so we skirted that area.

We talked to some guys in a B-24 squadron who had flown some missions over France. They told us that the flak was so thick they could have walked on it. The stuff we encountered around Ferrara and Verona were probably the heaviest that we saw. The sky resembled dark clouds in front of us.

August 1
We destroyed a heavy highway bridge at Balossa, Italy. We encountered no flak, always a good thing.

August 3
France at last! We figured we'd get there sooner or later, most likely sooner. We tried to hit a rail viaduct at Breil, but clouds covered primary and alternate targets, forcing us to return to base with our bombs still aboard. Even our alternate target was obscured. Weather wasn't helping us eliminate our assigned targets.

I don't recall for sure what our alternate target might have been, probably a bridge. We usually had alternate targets only when we expected to encounter weather in the main target area.

One thing we were cautioned against was not to take out targets of opportunity. If we saw other targets in the area, bombing them was verboten because we might have been taking out something intended for later Allied use. They wanted us to be accurate and take out only specifically assigned targets.

August 4

Our targets were at Nice, France, and Sori, Italy, but both were weathered in. The weather forecast had been correct, and by the time we got to the target the goldarn things were closed in and we couldn't see a thing. We had to return to base with our bombs and we didn't like to do that.

For some reason or other, after D-Day we all had a new impetus, a real shot of adrenalin. We were ready to go, and when we couldn't or didn't obliterate a target, we just felt terrible, really bad, much differently than we'd felt before.

When we got back to base, the ground crew unloaded the bombs.

August 8

On our third mission into France, the German gunners got to us. We were shot down over Avignon.

What we had seen happening to other planes on other missions had now happened to us, opening the door to an incredible adventure.

We were shot down on August 8, captured a few days later, and were prisoners of the Germans until August 19th. That's where I got my subtitle, *Eleven Days Running*. Maybe that title wasn't completely accurate, since we were in German custody for eight of those days and certainly weren't doing much running!

6.
ASSAULT ON AVIGNON

On the morning of August 8, 1944, we were scheduled for a mission and attended our pre-flight briefing at 6:30 in the morning, as usual. That gave us time to get things arranged, planes all set, and everything in order before take-off. Our mission that day was to bomb the railroad marshalling yards at Avignon, just north of Marseilles in southern France. I had volunteered for that mission, my 30th overall, and it turned out to be my last.

We loaded up and took off. As we neared the French coast, we were attacked by Me-109's (Messerschmitts). Our fighter plane cover on prior missions had been P-47s but they had been replaced on that mission with P-51s. The newer planes were better suited at the altitudes we generally flew and we were glad to have them with us. Our escorts immediately took off to intercept the enemy fighters. The P-51s dropped their wing fuel tanks, making the planes more maneuverable, and went to work. Meanwhile, our bomber squadron continued toward the target.

We only had two or three significant encounters with German fighter planes. Our own escort fighters would peel off and go after any enemy planes that came after us. Such was the case on our very last mission, but even then the enemy fighters didn't get to us.

The German forces were running low on fuel, thanks in part to our attacks on their supply points. That may have accounted for us not having a lot of contact or even seeing enemy fighter planes very often. Later in the war, the Germans could hardly get their planes off the ground for lack of fuel.

The crew with whom I flew on our mission to Avignon
Front Row (L-R): Joe Maywald, Gene Carman, Ed Weaver
Back Row (L-R): Unknown, John Sequenz, Richard Makoviac,
Anthony Citara

As we approached the target, we could see that flak had gotten pretty intense in front of us. We weren't expecting much resistance, but the intelligence at our pre-flight briefing must have been out-of-date. The Germans were pretty cagy with their arms movements. The air defense at Avignon was much more than we expected.

The lead plane opened its bomb bay doors and we did, too. His bombs dropped and so did ours. I stretched out over the bombsight to watch our bombs fall just as our plane took a direct hit, almost totally disabling it. But Joe Maywald and Ed Weaver, the pilot and copilot respectively, did a masterful job bringing us safely down in a meadow. I had minor shrapnel wounds but the rest of the crew escaped unscathed.

As a matter of fact, on all the missions I flew, there were few personnel injuries among my crew or any other crew I accompanied. All told, the injuries incurred during my flight missions included, other than myself, the observer who died from a shrapnel wound to the neck, and the tail-gunner P.A. Reed who was killed.

When we were hit, I couldn't believe how calm I felt. I had a clipboard on my lap and when I got hit, it felt as though someone had slapped my wrist. A piece of flak had hit my ring and ricocheted into my little finger. At the same time, I got a gash on my leg from another piece of shrapnel that, luckily, just grazed my thigh. I didn't realize I'd been hit there even though there was quite a bit of blood. I thought it all came from my finger.

Our plane had gotten the worst of it. Joe and Ed managed to put our crippled plane down in an open field. Fortunately for us, the plane didn't catch fire or explode when we crashed—Joe had switched off all power just before touchdown to minimize sparks.

Once we had slid to a stop, we did all the things we'd been trained to do when forced down in enemy territory. We destroyed all the valuable technology to prevent it from falling into enemy hands. I pulled out my .45 pistol and shot my Norden bombsight, which was like shooting a brother, a tough thing to do.

The bombsight had a gyro inside that was spinning at 30,000 rpm. Although the gyro was inside a metal case, I expected parts to fly through the case and hit me. Thankfully, that didn't happen. The gyro sputtered and made a lot of funny noises, but all the parts stayed inside. Nothing came out through the case.

Meanwhile, Joe and Ed took care of a bunch of sensitive stuff in the cockpit, instruments and whatever else they thought should not fall into enemy hands. The only thing I had to worry about was my bombsight.

7.
ON THE RUN

We got out of the plane, knowing we were in enemy territory. We expected the Germans to surround us at any moment, but didn't see anybody. We saw a trail alongside the field with bushes on either side. We all got down on our haunches and ran from the plane to the bushes. We looked up and down that trail to make sure no one was in sight. Then, one by one, we dashed across the trail to the bushes on the other side. There was a copse or grove of trees beyond the bushes that looked like it would offer pretty good cover. We were trying to hide from the enemy, so anything that would give us cover seemed like a good idea. We dashed for those trees.

As we were running for the trees, we heard dogs off in the distance. We thought, *Oh God, they've got dogs after us*. Fortunately, those dogs must not have been dogs of war. We never saw them, just heard them barking.

By that time, my ring finger had turned black. The ring had been dented from the shrapnel impact and pinched off my circulation. We each had an escape kit and in it was a metal saw that was about three inches long. It had the sharpest teeth you could imagine. Joe Maywald used his saw to cut the ring off my finger.

The escape kit had an amazing amount of stuff in it. We had morphine and very modest first-aid supplies in our kits. Each kit also included a kind of chocolate bar, a highly concentrated energy food. And finally, the kit had a map of southern France and several francs, the currency of the realm. All that stuff was in a little kit not much bigger than a cigarette pack. A great deal of thought had gone into its conception—lots of needs were met in an incredibly small package.

A day later I happened to brush the tip of my nose with my hand and felt something sharp and rough. Checking carefully, I found three very small pieces of Plexiglas imbedded in my nose and removed them.

My finger bled like fury, losing a lot of blood. After awhile, I told Joe I had to go find a farm house to get some medical attention. There had to be someone around there. I said, "Just sit tight and I'll be back."

He said, "No way. I'm going with you." He just wouldn't let me go alone.

As we started out I remembered that my wallet had lots of pictures and personal information. We had been told in general information sessions that it was best to keep such information out of enemy hands. My wallet and its contents may still be under a rock in a remote French field.

We hadn't gone far from where we were when we came to a little rise, just high enough that we couldn't see over it. Joe and I headed in that direction while the rest of our crew stayed hidden in the trees. Just beyond that rise we saw a farm house, a very small, typical French farm house. I say "typical French," but many farm houses in Europe looked very similar so it could have been anywhere. The house was a very small, one-story building with a little overhang front porch.

We went to the door and I knocked. An elderly woman came to the door and she was frightened. She was shaking. We could see her whole body just trembling. She was as big around as she was tall and absolutely scared to death.

In my best high school French, I said, "Nous sommes soif et faim, j'ai mal a me main." We're hungry, we're thirsty, and I've hurt my hand.

She replied, "Non, non, non." No, no, no, she said, pointing to where she said we could get help and away from her.

We couldn't see another house, but there was a very distinct trail that led from her house along a curve around some trees. We started walking along the trail, looking back at her occasionally. She kept pointing and motioning with her hand, and we understood that she was trying to direct us. Once we got around the curve, we saw another farmhouse.

We went to that house and in it were a man and three women. I never understood their relationship; I'm sure one of the women was the man's wife but which one never became clear to me. They were most gracious and attended to my wounds right away, as best they could. The man went out and retrieved the rest of our crew from where they were hiding in the trees. Then they fed us and I know that they had to take food out of their own mouths to feed our crew of six. They gave us some homemade bread, a round loaf about an inch-and-a-half thick and eight or 10 inches across. That bread was excellent, had a wonderful flavor. They also served us a very good soup with potato chunks in it.

The house had a lean-to on the side. Immediately outside the kitchen door and against the wall was a cabinet with a wash stand, sitting on what looked like a burlap rug. The man looked at me and smiled. He said, "The Boche never found this." Boche is a French derogatory term for German soldiers.

He pulled the cabinet and rug away, revealing a trapdoor leading to his wine cellar. I wasn't too much into wines at that time or any alcoholic beverages for that matter, but I can tell you that the wine was good, whatever it was, and very welcome.

They told us how to get in touch with the Maquis, the French underground, giving us directions. By then, it was getting toward dusk as we started out. It began to rain, just a drizzly, misty kind of rain. Richard Makoviac, our waist gunner, had on a jacket, the only one on our crew who had one, and he insisted that I wear it. He said, "You're hurt and you need this. Take it!" He would not let me refuse.

We followed directions given to us and came to a group of trees, where we spent the night. It rained throughout the night and we didn't sleep a whole lot. I think we may have dozed off and on. The ground was our bed but we stood in the trees through the night.

Paratrooper Dies, Two Fliers Reported Missing

Four Servicemen Listed as Wounded; Injuries Fatal to Pfc. Thorington

Seven more Flint war casualties were reported today — a paratrooper who died of wounds in France, two fliers missing in action and four servicemen wounded, three in France and one in Saipan. One was wounded for the second time.

They are:

Dead—Pfc. Benjamin F. Thorington.

Missing—2nd Lt. Erwin E. Carman, Staff Sgt. Raymond E. Fisher.

B. Thorington   Carman

Flint Journal, Sunday, August 21, 1944

Second Lt. Erwin E. Carman, bombardier - navigator with a Twelfth Air Force Mitchell group based on Corsica, has been missing in action over France since Aug. 8, his wife, Mrs. Elsie A. Carman, 1019 N. Stevenson St., has been notified.

Lt. Carman's advanced navigation training was received at Coral Gables, Fla., and his bombing training at Carlsbad, N. M. He was sent to Greenville, S. C., for further combat training before going overseas in May.

He participated in 29 missions over Italy and Southern France, from June 2 to Aug. 8, when he failed to return to his base.

After graduation from Northern High School in 1936, Lt. Carman was employed at Chevrolet in the parts distribution office. He has a son, Robert, at home.

Flint Journal, Sunday, August 21, 1944 (concluded)

Very early in the morning we heard a disturbance off in the distance. I said to Joe, "I've got to see what that is. Maybe we can get some help." We hoped it would be the Maquis but feared it might be Germans.

He said again, "Not alone," and we warily started off together.

The rest of the crew stayed behind and Joe and I crawled through the brush. We came to a place where there was a log lying across some bushes, offering us some cover from whoever was making the noise We peeked over the log and off in the distance we could see a lone figure, an elderly man. He was picking up faggots, limbs and branches and what have you, and bundling them. I don't know if they were for sale later or for his personal use in making a fire. We watched him for a long time to make sure he was alone.

Finally, I stood up and called to him. He reacted like the old lady—he started to shake all over. But he came over to us. When he realized we were Allies and that I had injuries, he said in French, "Wait, just wait and I'll bring help."

We were afraid that he would turn us in to the Germans, but there really wasn't anything else we could do except trust him. We knew there were Germans somewhere around us; at least we suspected they were around us.

Meanwhile, we wondered if we should move on and try to find the Maquis that our friends at the farmhouse had told us about. As it turned out, this older fellow had gone into a village about a mile or so from where we were. When he came back 45 minutes or so later, there must have been 35 or 40 other people with him. We thought, *Oh God, we are gone now!*

They also brought along with them a panel truck with solid sides and burlap over where the back windows had been.

One of the fellows in the group looked pretty scruffy, but presented himself as the local surgeon. He had a pair of rusty pliers, and I mean *rusty*. He removed the bandage and took the flak out of my finger with those pliers. One of the other Frenchmen took that piece of flak, spit on it, and threw it away. I wanted that piece of flak for a souvenir, but it was gone.

The Frenchmen wanted us to get out of our uniforms and get into different clothes to blend in better with the local folks. We all objected to that. If we were caught in civilian clothes and without our dog tags, we could have been treated as spies and shot. We didn't like that idea. They understood and went along with it.

They had us get into the truck—there was a bench on either side—and drove us into a very small village. All of a sudden we began hearing voices speaking German. We *knew* that we'd been had, but there wasn't much we could do about it at that point.

Our driver got out of the truck, went around, up on the sidewalk, and into one of the few buildings there. Soon he came out, talking to a German soldier. I peeked through the burlap on the back door, watching what was going on, knowing our driver would probably bring the German over to the truck. The Frenchman smiled happily and slapped the German soldier on the shoulder. The soldier smiled back, said something, and then left. Our driver came back to the truck and off we went again.

We were relieved, to say the least. *We've got it made now*, we thought.

He drove us about a mile out of town. When we came around a sharp bend, the driver turned off the dirt road. He went up a hill, and on top of the hill were some trees and a corncrib. There were no other buildings, just the corncrib and that's where we stayed overnight.

The family who had fed us earlier had given us bread to take with us. I had a piece of that bread in my breast pocket. That night as we were sleeping, a rat crawled across my chest headed for that bread! He was hungry. I *knew* that rat was going to bite me but he didn't.

The next morning, we woke up early. There were two men from the French group who had stayed with us. Those guys said, "Don't worry about breakfast. That'll come."

Soon some of the other Frenchmen arrived with a flatbed truck. They had some sort of storage tank just behind the driver's compartment outside the cab with a burner below it. That arrangement generated a gas from burning some sort of fuel in that tank, and that's what powered the truck. I don't know how it worked and they couldn't explain it to me.

On the truck bed they had several things they had taken from our plane: a bright yellow, eight-man life raft. They had it sitting on the back of this truck, inflated and in plain view for everyone in the world to see, including the Germans. They also had the machinegun from the nose of our airplane. If they had tried to fire it, whoever pulled the trigger would have been injured or killed; the recoil would have gotten him. They had quite a few other things from our plane.

The raft would accommodate eight people, so it was good-sized. They wanted us to get on the back of flatbed truck with this brilliant, yellow, inflated life raft. Remember, we were trying to be inconspicuous and hide from the Germans.

We were reluctant to do that, but we figured (hoped?) they knew what they were doing. They drove us to the center of their local Maquis headquarters, on a hilltop—a curious place to put an underground headquarters! There was a house and a lot of fences in the area.

One of the Maquis spoke very good English. We asked him what was going on and did we have any chance of getting out of there. He couldn't give us a real answer, except to say that the Boche were all around us. They gave us a light breakfast of bread and cheese, both delicious.

We stayed with the Maquis all that day and that evening we went to another farmhouse some distance away. That farmhouse was a beautiful old building, all stone, a long, two-story structure. Alongside the living quarters opposite the kitchen area was a breezeway leading to another part of the building, an animal barn.

While we were there, a goat walked through the breezeway and right into the house. The house had a Dutch door leading from the breezeway, but both the top and bottom halves were open. The floor in the kitchen was dirt. In fact, all the floors on the ground level of the house were dirt. But everything was immaculate; the house was exceptionally well-kept. Everything was neat and in order and in place. The lady of the house shooed the goat out very casually.

They had a radio on and what sounded like the Voice of America playing. I've often wondered what happened to those people, because the Germans could have easily heard the radio and discovered that the occupants were harboring fugitives: us! As things developed later, the Germans knew the family had sheltered us.

Early the next morning, they fixed bread and cheese for us—we were starting to notice a trend. They also gave us coffee that I knew they couldn't afford to give out. It was strong but very good.

After breakfast we heard a rat-a-tat-tat in the distance. We knew machinegun fire when we heard it and that was machinegun fire. I went to the door, actually just an opening in the breezeway. I looked down along the wall of the house and way off in the distance I could see a line of German soldiers. Each had a rifle or machinegun. I don't know what the shooting was about. The important thing was that Germans were marching toward us.

The crew and I got out of the house and ran, keeping the house between ourselves and the Germans. We broke all the Olympic sprinting records, headed for the nearby trees! As we ran through the trees, we routed a feral sow and three piglets and, boy, she was big, must have been three feet tall and 300 pounds. She came out of the brush with those piglets behind her and she just kept going, running away from us thank goodness!

We kept on running but could hear the Germans behind us. We ran up a hill and decided that we were probably going to be captured. If so, we thought it'd be a good idea not to be armed. We all carried handguns, .45 automatics, which we hid in the shrubbery. We hoped to stay hidden in the brush until dark and then try to get away. Where we'd go or what we would do, we had no idea.

We heard the Germans go past us, lower down the hill, as we lay in the brush. We all breathed a sigh of relief. They'd missed us!

But the Germans were smarter than we had given them credit. They turned around and began marching back toward us, spreading out from the bottom of the hill to the top, beating the brush as they came. As they got closer and closer, I could feel my body rise off the ground with each heartbeat. I could hear my heart and I just knew that anyone who got within 100 feet of me could hear it, too. It was that strong.

About the time back in boot camp when I tried to bayonet my friend from Flint, the lead NCO was a little put out with me. I stopped short of saying, "He was not a happy camper." The lead NCO's name was Nadio, and he was funny. Nadio was almost as big around as he was tall, but solid as a rock. He looked fat but, when you touched him, it was like touching a post. He was the toughest guy there was on barracks, orderlies, and that kind of stuff but the softest heart you ever saw. If you knew how to get around him, and you could find out pretty easily, he wasn't nearly as bad as he seemed. He barked harshly, but he was quite a guy. He just wanted you to do the smart thing for your own protection. Whatever you were assigned to do, he wanted you to do it right.

When we were being chased by the Germans we heard gunfire. I dropped to the ground and took cover. The first thought that flashed through my mind was, *Boy, Nadio would be proud of me now! I had hit the dirt in a split second and he would have smiled.*

With the Germans drawing steadily nearer, the roar of my heartbeat was deafening. Expecting the worst, I rationalized that I wouldn't even hear the shot that killed me. I uttered three words: Help me God.

Immediately a feeling of peace took control of my mind. I knew without question that God was in control. I have never before or since experienced such calm.

The Germans were getting very close, and we could hear their footsteps. Weaver was next to me, on my left. Ed stood with his hands up and yelled, "We're Americans."

When Ed got up, I got up, too. The German soldier in front of me was pointing his rifle at me. He looked at me and said, "Américan?"

I said, "Oui, nous sommes American." Yes, we are American.

The German soldier said, "Vive América!" Long live America!

The date was August 11, 1944, three days following our plane crash.

8.
CAPTURED!

The Army Air Corps had established a protocol that, for flyers that were captured by the enemy, the lowest non-commissioned rank would be sergeant. They established that policy because any Allies who were captured were treated much better if they were a sergeant or higher. Following that protocol, we declared to our captors that all of our enlisted crew truly were sergeants.

The German soldiers rounded us up and marched us to the bottom of the hill. Some of the soldiers had big bags containing who-knows-what, which they loaded onto members of our crew to carry. Me they gave nothing, probably because of my wounds. I had a terrible headache, a headache that wouldn't quit. The Germans gave me medication for it that relieved the problem in short order.

They marched us to a flatbed truck with an arrangement of seats running crosswise on the bed. They had us get onto the truck with six Germans guarding us as we rode.

We started down a road until we came around a curve. On the inside of the curve was an area maybe 20x50 feet that was relatively clear. The Germans had also rounded up 14 French members of the Maquis, and were holding them there. One of the Maquis was actually Portuguese, a young man, and he tried his best to get us to say that he was part of our crew. We didn't realize at the time why he was asking that, but we knew that it wouldn't take the Germans any time at all to see through that falsehood. The young man couldn't speak English for one thing and he wasn't dressed as we were.

We moved again and rounded a curve about 100 feet past the hostages when we again heard the rat-a-tat-tat of machinegun fire. We knew the Germans had executed the 14 Maquis. The Maquis were aiding us—they were the French resistance—they were on our side. The man I mentioned earlier who spoke such good English was a member of that group of 14.

You must understand that we weren't wearing traditional uniforms, so those soldiers weren't sure who we were except that we were opposing forces. The guards on that truck were not the same ones who had captured us. They were very stern-faced and did not try to communicate with us.

On an impulse, I said to them in French, "Nous sommes American." We are American.

That had an immediate, positive effect. There were smiles and chatter, with no further sign of animosity.

The truck stopped at a tiny village where the guards were going to buy snacks and they indicated that they would get some for us. We had money from our escape kits and they accepted it, bought us grapes and even gave us change from the francs we had given them.

The Germans got back on the truck and took off again, taking us on quite a long ride. At one point, we heard two rifle shots off in the distance. The German officer (I don't know his rank) ordered the small convoy we were in to stop. Then he ordered two of his men to scout and find out what was going on while we stayed there. Soon, we heard two more shots.

When the scouts came back, I can still see the dramatic replay in my mind's eye. One of the scouts stood in front of his commander at stiff attention, saluted, and reached into his pocket. Then, with a very deliberate motion, he lifted a wallet up very high, brought it back down, and handed it to his commander. We just knew that the scouts had killed whoever had fired the shots heard earlier. That gave me a strange feeling. I don't know why that incident sticks out so clearly in my mind, but it does.

We resumed our travel until we got to Digne, France, to the Ermitage Hotel. That's where we were to be quartered. During "check-in," the German officer, who queried us there, asked if we wanted to be separated, officers from enlisted, or if we wanted to room together. We chose the latter. They put us in a basement room, a long room with barred windows at one end, a single door, and three beds. That worked out fine.

Immediately before getting to the hotel itself, the road leading there was quite curvy. As we came around one curve, there sat an American tank that had been burned out, all rusted over. In the front of it was a hole that looked to be about 12 inches across. As we continued, at the top of the hill there sat a German 85 mm howitzer with its barrel leveled in the direction of the tank. That gun apparently had been what had gotten that American tank as it came around the curve.

Once we got to the hotel, I had to use the latrine and I had a devil of a time explaining to the German soldiers what I wanted. Finally, somewhere in the dark recesses of my mind I came up with the term "WC", for water closet. That's a universal term and I had tried everything else I knew to say, except WC. When I said that, the guard's eyes widened, he knew exactly what I meant, and he took me to the latrine.

The day after we were captured, our captors took me to the German hospital and took care of my finger and leg wounds. The German doctors were just as solicitous and nice as they could be. The bone in the little finger between my knuckle and first joint had been crushed by the piece of shrapnel. They took care of my finger, putting it in a cast so that it stuck straight out. The cast actually covered my ring finger, too. They sent me back to the cell or room where my fellow crewmen were being held.

We were interrogated many times. I don't remember that we ever had contact with the SS branch of Hitler's forces, with one possible exception. There were two hatchet-faced, sallow-complexioned fellows with deep-set, dark eyes. They were both wearing civilian clothes, so I'm not sure of their ranks or even if they were military. They had absolutely black hair and eyebrows. Those two men interrogated us and threatened us with all sorts of inhumanities if we didn't cooperate. Fortunately, we saw them for only a short time before they were gone.

During one of our interrogations, a German officer with an absolutely beautiful uniform came before us. I don't know his rank either, but his uniform was very impressive. It was soft grey with brass buttons, epaulets, and red trim. The lapel had been turned back just so. He wore a monocle, a mustache, and one of those German caps with a high crown. His name could have been Colonel Klink from *Hogan's Heroes* TV fame, an exact Hollywood-type German officer right out of Central Casting. Frankly, we were a little amused that everything about him was so perfect.

He kept telling us, "Answer dis or you vill be shot!"

As with the other interrogators, we gave him our name, rank, and serial number, the only things required by the Geneva Convention. While not satisfied, they all accepted our responses.

During one interrogation, several German NCOs were questioning us in an office. On the wall behind their desk was a map of Italy, and on the map were lines where they must have thought the German and Allied forces were. They had a line drawn to show where they thought the front was located, Axis to the north and Allies to the south. I knew the line should have been shown much further north. So did the rest of my group.

As the NCOs were talking, I told the soldier behind the desk, "That line should be further north."

"Vas?" What?

I said, "The line is way up here," pointing to where I thought the Allies had advanced.

"Nein," he insisted. No. "Line is here," pointing to the line on the map.

They would not believe that the Allied advance had been so rapid. I probably shouldn't have said what I said, but I just couldn't resist the temptation.

That incident brought back memories. In 1935 or1936, we had a German family in our neighborhood who had immigrated to the States a few years earlier and whose kids attended my high school. They believed that the Germans had won WWI—that's what they'd been taught in German schools.

One of the guards at the hotel spoke fairly good English. I tried to get him to find some way to get us out of there. We tried everything we could think of along those lines. It became nonsensical after a while, but we had to try. He listened but would not cooperate.

We had to leave the room occasionally, for instance when we took a shower or had to use the latrine. The room they took us to for those functions was just a big, open room. The shower wasn't even in a corner of the room; it was well out from the walls. The room had a drain in the floor, and on each side of the drain were slightly raised footprints in the concrete. If you stood on those footprints, you could shower, eliminate, whatever you needed to do. You just pulled the overhead chain to flush or run water for a shower. That one spot served as a toilet *and* a shower, quite an efficient system.

For our daily showers or to go to the bathroom, the English-speaking guard went with us.

On Aug 15, the Germans decided they needed to move us to a regular prison camp. They arranged for a convoy to leave on the morning of the third day, very early, before dawn. They loaded us onto a flatbed truck again, under guard of course, and started out of the city.

We hadn't gotten very far, not even to the outskirts of the city, when we came to an overhead railroad crossing. The French Maquis were on that overpass and opened fire on our convoy below. As I've said before, the Maquis were valiant people, but they did some things that didn't seem to involve good, deep thinking (remember the hilltop secret headquarters?). When they opened fire they had no regard for who might have been in that convoy. One of their rifle shots hit the truck we were in but didn't hit anyone. Elsewhere in the convoy, there were six German soldiers wounded and one killed.

The Germans turned the convoy around and retreated. But instead of going back to the Ermitage they took us to a fort within the city. That fort had thick walls all the way around it that were 10-12 feet high. I don't really have a feel for the dimensions of the fort as far as area is concerned.

Inside the walls were several buildings. We were quartered in the headquarters building, which also held the kitchen and a mess hall for the German soldiers. They put us in a big room that had straw strewn on the floor, and that served as our bedding. The room had a kind of picnic table with benches at which we could eat. Otherwise, there was nothing else in the room.

One of the guards gave us a deck of cards. We played euchre when we weren't being interrogated or otherwise occupied. Everything we did we did in that one room, except showers and going to the bathroom.

A couple of things I remember about that room: The windows had no glass, not even a frame, just bars. The door to the room was huge, obviously handmade, probably four inches thick and close to four feet across. It was a big door and, for Europe, a tall door.

The door had a big keyhole, just huge, maybe two by five inches. I never saw the key they used to open the door and can't imagine what it must have looked like. I could hear the key being used but I never did see it.

We hadn't been in the room 30 minutes before I heard a clatter at the keyhole. I thought someone might be coming in, but there was just clatter and then silence. I went over, found a piece of paper in the keyhole, which I took out and opened. On it, written in French, was a greeting from the women who served as maids and cooks. That was their way of bringing us good cheer, telling us to keep the faith, and that everything was going to be alright.

If the Germans had found that piece of paper, I'm sure those girls would have been killed. I kept that piece of paper for the longest time, but eventually lost it.

Our primary guard there, the one who spoke English, was very pleasant. We got the impression that all the Germans at this site were probably there on R&R, rest and relaxation. I'm certain that most if not all of them had come from the Russian front. They were glad to be where they were and not at the front.

The next morning the guard came in and apologized for having to cut us down from three meals a day to two. He said it had to be done because rations were scarce and we were not fighting, so we didn't need as much food. I should mention that I like soup and that's what we were getting. It was very good. The bread they gave us with our soup was a dark, round loaf about two inches thick and it, too, was more than tasty.

A little later, they moved us into another building but still within the fort compound. The back of that building served as part of the wall of the fort. Probably 25 feet from that building was a latrine with a number of holes. While I was in there doing my business one day, a woman came in and sat down two holes away from me. That gave me a pucker that wouldn't quit!

On August 15, Andy Citara had become ill and the Germans took him to the hospital, where he received professional, compassionate care for three days before bringing him back to camp.

Early on the morning of August 16 we heard aircraft off in the distance. There were P-47s on a special mission and one of them dive-bombed a bridge inside the walls of the fort. As the pilot dove and released his ordnance, it looked as though the bomb would come right down our throats. We thought we were going to be killed by our own military.

But the bomb made a direct hit on the bridge, only about 100 feet from us. The concussion shook the walls and broke windows. It put a crater in the bridge, which had been constructed totally of brick and stone. But even after the bomb hit, the bridge still had enough room to drive a small cart over it. It hadn't been damaged that badly, which says something about its construction many years ago.

After the bomb hit, we heard more aircraft noise. We looked up into the sky and there came B-25s by the jillions. I don't know how many squadrons had been put together for that formation, but it had to be several. One of the German soldiers said, "Ach, so many!"

The planes went on by us, apparently headed for targets farther north.

After the attack, the Germans moved us back to the big room with the barred windows in the headquarters building.

The next morning, August 17, the Germans decided that they would try once again to move us to a prison camp. We got ambushed at exactly the same place. When the gunfire erupted, the truck we were in ran off the edge of the road, a 10-12 foot drop. The truck flipped over on its side and we slid down the embankment. Some of us were bruised but, fortunately, nobody got seriously injured.

There was a German with us on the truck, dressed in civilian clothes, who spoke perfect English. We were tired of being shot at by the French—they were opening up on just anyone. The fleeting thought crossed our minds that, if we had guns we could shoot back. Once again the Maquis killed one German soldier and I'm not sure if any were wounded in that second fracas.

Again, the convoy turned around and took us back. That ended our foray to other places. They didn't try to relocate us after that.

The following day we noticed two or three different things: Off in the distance and getting closer we heard the boom of heavy artillery, coming from the south. Outside our room, German soldiers would walk by the barred window occasionally. As they passed, they made sure they had our attention. Then they'd spit on the ground and say, "Hitler!"

We had had earlier indications that Hitler wasn't being held in the highest esteem by some of the German soldiers. But it wasn't an overt thing, nothing expressed openly. When the Allied artillery got closer and closer to the fort, they must have seen the handwriting on the wall and became more open about their feelings. Maybe they wanted us to know that they were disgusted with Hitler and hoped we'd remember that when the war ended and our roles were reversed.

I couldn't tell you how many of them walked by our window and said, "Hitler! Ptooie!" I suspect they knew that the end was near and they'd better do what they could to ingratiate themselves with us. I have to say that we were treated extremely well by the Germans.

9.
RESCUED

On the morning of August 19, we heard machinegun and howitzer fire. In late afternoon, the Germans moved us to a more secure area of the fort. After a while, the bombardment got very close. The German captain, who commanded the garrison in which we were being held, came to me and said, "I want to talk to you."

I was open to any discussion so he took me aside and said, "I'm not going to surrender to the French, to the British, and certainly not to the Maquis. But I will surrender to you."

I said words to the effect, "I'm all for that!"

We shook hands and he said, "Come with me."

We went to the wall of the fort where there were steps up to a little platform that served as a guard station. We went up onto the platform and on the other side of the wall stood an American infantry captain, a French officer, a British officer (I don't know the ranks of the latter two), and several Maquis. I showed the American officer my dog tags and explained my agreement with the German captain. The American and French captains agreed that the surrender could take place as the German officer had requested.

The German captain and I walked down the stairs and into the building, where I asked the German officer to gather all of his men, six officers and 60 enlisted men.

He asked me, "What do I do?"

I replied that he should give me his pistol. I took his Luger and put it on the floor. "Tell your men to put their weapons there, too."

They had rifles, pistols, and bayonets, a long and short one of the latter. They placed them all on the pile. I later kicked myself for not keeping the captain's Luger as a souvenir. But I did retrieve a soldier's belt complete with an embossed buckle, and a long and a short bayonet in their scabbards. The buckle had an embossed an inscription that said ''*Got mit uns*'', God with us. My son has that belt.

We went outside and at that point somebody opened a huge gate that led through the outer wall out of the compound. Outside the gate sat an American tank with an Army sergeant driving and another sergeant walking ahead of the tank, serving as a guide. Boy, did they look good to us! They looked great!

We were about to leave to find the American officer when the German captain turned to Joe Maywald, inquiring about the health and wellbeing of himself and his men. His tone of voice indicated his concern. He clearly feared some kind of retaliation from the French.

We knew that if we turned him loose at that point and let the French people into the fort, it would have been disastrous. The Maquis probably would have killed or badly wounded every one of the prisoners. The French we had met had a deep-seated hatred of the Germans.

Joe said, "You're with us and we'll stand between you and them," them being the French, British, and Maquis. I echoed Joe's sentiments, that the captain had surrendered to us, he was *our* prisoner, and we would do our best to take care of him and his men.

As it turned out, we did have to intervene on behalf of the Germans, because everyone, especially the Maquis, were after them. Only our intercession prevented slaughter. The Maquis had had it up to their eyebrows with German treatment and were anxious to take their revenge. We had a very scary experience keeping the Maquis off the Germans, until the allied troops came in force and the prisoners were turned over to American forces.

A little bit later, in an open compound in which all the German prisoners were being kept, I visited with Hans Bergman, one of our German guards at the Ermitage Hotel. There were no problems. The Germans were behaving themselves and the guards of all nationalities were behaving themselves.

The German commander had given me the cashbox for his unit. In it were a whole bunch of francs, keys, unit records, and what have you. When I first got the cashbox, I expected to find the key to that big door, but it wasn't in there. If it had been, I'd probably still have it today.

The keys were for many other locks and a wine cellar—I checked that out at my first opportunity. The door to the wine cellar was at ground level and inside was a ramp running down. The wine cellar looked like a dugout cellar. At the bottom I found a narrow walkway with racks for bottles on either side. Every freaking bottle of wine had been broken! They'd broken every single bottle, so there was no wine with which to celebrate.

While we were imprisoned in the fort, right outside our quarters there were two gorgeous German Police dogs, German Shepherds, working dogs. I noticed that one particular guard was with the dogs nearly all the time. The camaraderie between him and the dogs became so obvious. I commented to him through this friend, the sergeant who spoke English, that I really appreciated him taking such good care of the dogs.

When the fort surrendered, the K-9 corporal brought the dogs and, with tears in his eyes, gave them to me. Before the corporal gave the dogs to me, he spoke to them in German, handed me the leash, and patted my hand. The dogs seemed to know exactly what the corporal was saying and signaling, because the dogs went with me and didn't cause me a bit of trouble.

So, there I was with those two German Shepherds, in wartime and not speaking German, which is the only thing the dogs understood. I wondered what I should do with the dogs. I pondered the problem for the longest time and eventually walked to the Ermitage Hotel with both dogs obediently at heel to see if I could find the American commander. I couldn't find him or anyone else who would take the dogs.

I commandeered a jeep, put the dogs in it, and drove back out to the prisoner camp. The dogs sat in the seat right beside me, just as calm and obedient as you please. I'll admit to being a little nervous about them, but they never bothered me in any way, shape, or form.

Back at camp, I returned the dogs to the K-9 corporal, not having any idea what he could do with them. I knew the dogs would probably be destroyed, but I just didn't know what else to do. The corporal seemed happy to see his dogs again, but at the same time must have realized what would happen to his K-9 companions.

That event has bothered me ever since. I just hate it that I had to give up those dogs, not knowing but fearing what their fate might be, yet I couldn't find anyone in the military who would take them. How unfortunate.

I turned over the cashbox and its contents to LTC Perry, the G2 (Intel) with the Texas 36th Infantry Division, and he gave me a receipt. We sat under a tree when this took place, very relaxed. I told him I'd write to his family when I got back to base, and I did.

I'm always amazed that all of this could have happened in just 11 days. It just blows my mind—an incredibly short time for so much to take place.

Hq. 7th Army
Office of A C of S, G-2

21 Aug 44

Received of 2nd Lt Erwin E.
Carman German mail Strong
box containing records, official
stamps and 39 669.30 francs
and 2 Reichsmarks

Lewis E. Levy
Lt Col J S C
asst G-2

Receipt for German Cashbox

10.
LEAVING THE WAR ZONE

When it came time to leave Digne, LTC Perry arranged for the crew to be transported south to the coastal headquarters. We got on an armed, flatbed truck that had a .50 caliber machinegun turret beside the driver, mounted above the cab. The co-pilot of the truck also served as the turret operator. The soldier manning the gun was very alert.

En route south, we heard shots off in the distance several times. When that happened, the SGT in the turret would swing his .50 immediately toward the sound of the shots. He was on it right away, ready to respond as needed. Apparently, none of the shots were aimed at us. The machine gunner told us that, on the way to the fort to rescue us, their advance had been so rapid that they had driven past several pockets of German soldiers and that those soldiers probably didn't know that the war was over for them. Thus, they were subject to fire at us if our paths crossed. Like the prison guards earlier with their map of Italy, they just couldn't believe they were losing the war.

We went to the coast, near the town of Saint Tropez. I have no idea the distance between that town and the fort in which we'd been held prisoner. We were on the coast for only a couple of days, awaiting transportation to get us back to our base.

I have several distinct memories of Saint Tropez. Among them are the vineyards with huge clumps of grapes on sturdy vines not over three feet tall. Also, every evening at five o'clock, a lone German observation plane flew over the town and waggled its wings. He was so regular that we could have set our watches. We called him "Five O'clock Jerry."

We were at St Tropez long enough to see "Five O'clock Jerry" twice. He flew something the size of a Taylorcraft, if you know something about planes, but it had an open cockpit. The pilot would waggle his wings and the guys on the ground would wave to him.

I don't remember how we got from the St. Tropez area back to Corsica, but we must have flown. I have an indistinct memory of landing at Corsica, but I couldn't swear to it. I can tell you for sure we didn't drive!

We stayed there for the better part of a week. Our quarters were back in the same building that housed the mess hall, on the second floor. I went to my cot but someone else had staked his claim. Boy did that make me feel expendable! Another thing they had done was put my duffle bag in storage. I got it back but it no longer contained my leather flight jacket. The guy who had taken my cot had also helped himself to my flight jacket. He had already removed my name, insignia, rank, and all that business. He gave it back. I had it for years but eventually lost track of it.

Once I'd been rescued, I didn't fly any more missions. At that time, there was an order to the effect that, if you had been taken prisoner, you were no longer required to perform combat and could be sent home. That was alright with me!

Missing Flint Flier Turns Up With 66 German Prisoners

9-1-44

A Flint flier who had been captured by 66 Germans in Southern France was safe at his base in Italy today—and with the 66 German prisoners to his credit.

Second Lt. Erwin E. Carman had been listed as missing in action over France since Aug. 8. The Mitchell bomber on which he was navigator-bombardier crash landed in Southern France, and the crew of 6 was joined by 15 French patriots. All of them fell into the hands of the Germans and were taken to a fort.

Lt. Carman

Soon, however, a large band of patriots began storming the fort, and the German commander called Lt. Carman, offering to surrender to the Flint flier rather than fall into the hands of the patriots.

So Lt. Carman and his crew turned their 66 prisoners over to American ground troops, and returned to their base in Italy.

His wife, Elsie, 1019 N. Stevenson St., who had nothing from the War Department regarding his status since he was reported missing learned from The Journal that he returned Thursday to his base in Italy. The news came in the following Associated Press dispatch from Rome:

"Six crewmen of an American Mitchell bomber returned to their base today to relate a story of capturing 6 German officers and 60 enlisted men who but a short time before were their captors.

"The bomber crash landed in Southern France, and the crew was joined by 15 French patriots, but all fell into German hands and were taken to a fort.

"When a strong patriot force began storming the fort, the German commander called Lt. Carman, the bombardier-navigator on the Mitchell, and offered to surrender to the Americans rather than fall into patriot hands.

"The Americans, with the consent of the French, accepted the surrender, disarmed the captives and turned them in."

Lt. Carman participated in 29 missions over Italy and Southern France, from June 2 to Aug. 8, when he failed to return to his base. After graduation from Northern High School in 1936, he was employed at Chevrolet. He has a son, Robert, at home.

Flint Journal, **September 1, 1944**

During navigation training, I learned to observe what was on the ground as we were flying to and from a mission. Occasionally in combat, I'd see a truck or something else interesting. I'd pinpoint the location and then give that information to our home base operator when we landed. They'd do whatever they thought was appropriate with that information.

When I came back under Allied control after having been a prisoner, one of the lieutenants in charge of the camp said, "You ought to come back as an observer." He must have thought I had a good eye for detail, but I had no interest in returning to combat in any capacity.

From Corsica we went to Naples, where we ex-prisoners stayed for a good week. We were again waiting for transportation, a liberty ship to take us and others back to the States. Our government had taken over fleets of cargo vessels and was retrofitting them for this purpose. They installed cots, mess halls, galleys, and so on for transporting troops. The James S. Parker was our ship.

Meanwhile, our quarters were in tents but very comfortable. After sleeping on straw or in the rain as we had done, we now lived in comparative luxury.

We had plenty of time to relax and take in some of the sights in Naples. I remember the open markets where all sorts of items were sold, from clothing and jewelry to food and artwork, all at attractive prices. We also went to a number of good restaurants and bars where we heard some very good music.

On one occasion we were at a bistro and the music being played there was just beautiful. Those musicians could take a mandolin and make it sing. There must have been 20 of us there when a mother and two daughters came into the bistro. They sat down and looked around the room. Finally, the mother came over and said to me in broken English, "We would like to invite you to dinner."

I thought, *Gee, what a nice gesture.*

I was all for it and went to dinner with the mother and her daughters. As it turned out, she intended to fix me up with one of her daughters, hoping she would marry an American and be able to leave Italy. I didn't know that until later.

That evening we had a great meal consisting of several courses. The Italians didn't have much, but they could make a wonderful meal out of almost nothing. When it came time for dessert, the mother asked if I would like wine with my peaches. That sounded pretty good. What she brought me was dessert compote with peaches in wine, and it was delicious, absolutely delicious.

Some of the best Italian food I'd ever had in my life came from Naples. They could make do with almost nothing. I especially enjoyed my evening with the Italian mother and her daughters, until it became obvious why they had chosen me. When they learned that I was married, they were very respectful and the evening ended pleasantly.

I told a member of my crew, Andy Citara, about that wonderful peach dessert. He laughed at me, saying, "We have that in the refrigerator at home all the time."

Andy told me that they'd take fruit cocktail, pour off the juice, and replace it with wine. That was a staple in their refrigerator, he told me. It must be some sort of Italian invention. What a delicious concoction.

Another time, we were at a mall in Naples where the whole ceiling area up above was an iron dome, a steel framework that at one time had held panes of glass. Though the mall had never been hit directly, bombs landed close enough that the concussion broke all the windows. All that remained was the steel framework.

There were kids all over the place with potbellies, starving and malnourished. Little kids, eight, nine, 10 years old, would say to us, "Hey meester, you wanna eat? You wanna dreenk? You wanna sleepa my seester?"

Things like that were just rampant.

A vendor at the mall had what he called a mantilla, a scarf made by an Italian woman that was absolutely beautiful, an outstanding piece of lace work. It made me think about my wife's grandmother in West Branch, Michigan, and thought about buying the scarf for her. I didn't buy it then for a reason that escapes me and when I made up my mind to go back and get it, it was gone.

In a European town of any size, they'd have a farmer's market. They displayed their wares on tables or even on the ground. I remember seeing one table that had tomato sauce displayed on it, and flies like you wouldn't believe all over the stuff. Many of the merchants spoke English, enough that I could communicate with them. I also spoke some French and that helped a lot. I asked the man at the table about the flies, expressing my concern.

He said, "No, the flies help. They help. We brush them away and then package it up."

He didn't explain how the flies helped.

He had everything from tomato sauce to take home or to put on your food if you wanted to eat there.

Many vendors in the mall were selling cameos that were beautiful. One of the vendors warned me that there were fakes among them and you had to know what to look for, or you could get taken. He spoke mostly in Italian and my French/Italian wasn't working too well, but I understood what he told me about some of them being fakes. What I couldn't pick up from him was just *how* to tell the fake cameos from the real ones, so I didn't buy any.

11.
STATESIDE AGAIN

It took us about a week to cross the Atlantic on the Parker, landing near Fort Dix, New Jersey.

When we docked, everyone grabbed their duffle bags to debark. However, I still had wounds and struggled with mine. I came down the gangplank, shuffling along and dragging my bag. A PFC stood at the bottom of the gangplank directing traffic and he yelled at me, "Come on, come on!" I was in uniform with my rank displayed, but that didn't seem to impress him. For the first time in my life, I had an inclination to pull rank. I wanted to tell him to shove it, but I didn't.

On the dock, they loaded us into a truck and took us to a barracks at Fort Dix. There were several soldiers assigned to the reception committee, or whatever they called it. In any event these troops met us at the dock and rode with us to the fort for processing. I asked a corporal how things were here in the States.

"They're okay," he replied, "except we have to eat canned bacon."

I guess everyone had their definition of hardship.

We stayed at Fort Dix for maybe a week.

The second night we were there, three of us decided to go to New York City, a place we'd never been before. We were oohing and aahing at all the tall buildings, just like typical tourists. We stopped at a saloon near Times Square called The Student Prince and took seats at the bar. This was in the early evening and the place was packed.

I had just finished reading in *The Reader's Digest*, a story about White Russia, and discussed it with my friends. We noticed that the bartender didn't wander too far away unless he had to wait on someone else. Pretty soon he joined in on our discussion. He was from White Russia!

"I'm going off duty in a little while," the bartender said. "What are you fellows doing for the evening?"

We told him we had nothing particular in mind; we just wanted to see New York.

"Just stick around until I get off," he said. "I'll take you around."

True to his word, he took us around the city. We went into a place called Diamond Jim's, a nightclub owned by Diamond Jim Brady. We went to at least three other clubs, and every club we went into it seemed that everybody knew our bartender friend. He introduced us to quite a few different people.

We went into one place in Greenwich Village, a below-ground-level place but quite large. They had a big entertainment area with a lady singer performing. Our bartender friend introduced us to the singer. Her name was Olga Winatka. She had a gorgeous voice, a soprano but with body, not shrill at all.

By the way, our bartender's name was Alex Pokra, and his brother had some sort of connection with the New York Philharmonic Orchestra. Alex didn't tell us this, but we soon surmised that he introduced new talent to the clubs and Olga was one of the newer ones. That must be how everyone in the entertainment world seemed to know Alex.

We spent the night at Alex's house. He was as patronizing and patriotic as he could be. He wanted us to see everything and showed us as much as he could in a very short time. We would never have seen most of the things he showed us otherwise.

The following day, we toured the city some more. That evening, we went to quite a number of hotels looking for a room but they all turned us down—no vacancy.

We wound up at the Commodore at 1st Avenue and 42nd Street, at Grand Central Station. I asked the desk clerk, "I guess this is unreasonable, but do you have a room for three servicemen?"

He looked at me for a second and then said, "Could you use a suite?"

The clerk charged us the single-room rate, but gave us a beautiful suite.

Every time I went to New York in later years, I always stayed at the Commodore.

From Fort Dix, the Army Air Corps sent me to El Paso, Texas. There I went to William Beaumont Hospital for treatment of my wounds. In the hospital, I saw guys who had every conceivable injury, from missing limbs, burns, you name it. There was one young fellow and, when I looked at him, I knew there was something different about him. I eventually realized that it was the tone or color of his skin. It was a healthy but abnormal pink. All visible flesh on him was that color and it had all been transplanted from other parts of his body.

Guys who had facial damage, such as missing ears, received ingenious treatment. The doctors would make two parallel cuts on a patient's back and leave a strip of skin in the center. When it healed, they'd cut the lower end off and move it up higher up the guy's back. Using that technique, they'd stair-step that strip up his back until they had it up on the side of the patient's head where they made a new ear.

If someone had burns on a finger, the doctors would make incisions in the patient's abdomen, insert the damaged finger, and leave it there until the body had formed new skin. At that point, the doctors would remove the finger from the patient's abdomen.

My wife came out to visit me at Beaumont hospital and got ill from seeing all the injured guys.

When I saw a doctor, he removed the cast from my hand and said, "You don't want your finger like that."

He took my finger and gave it a snap. I wanted to hit him! The finger is still stiff and immobile, but it's curled rather than pointing straight out. He was right in what he did, but I just didn't like his method.

Between surgeries and inspections at Beaumont Hospital, we had a lot of free time. We'd go into downtown El Paso and visit the local joints. That was interesting. Outside of El Paso was a place called El Ranchotel. They had not only the motel and swimming pool, they also had horses. They had riding and riding instruction. The hotel had a nice bonfire going every night, and it was the most pleasant thing to sit next to that fire under the Texas skies. Way off in the distance we could see mountains.

One night we decided we'd ride to the foothills of the mountains. We got some horses and mounted up. None of us had been on horseback in quite some time. We rode, and we rode, and we rode, and we rode some more but we never got to the foothills. We got so sore and were so tired. We turned the horses around. The horses knew where they were going and off they went. They were going home and we were just along for the ride. The horses were headed for the barn and, if we wanted to come along, that was alright. If we didn't, that would have been okay, too. We hung on for dear life. Crazy!

El Ranchotel was such a lively place to be. Almost anything you'd care to do you could do there, but I tried to be restrictive in the things I did. We spent a lot of time there away from the hospital.

We went across the border into Juarez many times. I think about that now as compared to then, and there's a vast difference. One time we were going to a restaurant. On the way, there were little kids who were eight, nine, ten years old and it brought back memories from my time in Naples. Here again, these little boys would ask us, "Hey senor, you wanna to eat? You wanna to dreenk? You wanna to sleep weeth my seester?"

These kids were saying the same things as the kids in Naples, but with a Spanish accent. They knew just enough English to convey their messages.

We usually drove across the Rio Grande when we went to Juarez. If we parked our car and left it for any length of time, we never knew if it would be there when we returned. What we'd do was pay a teenager to watch our car. We learned very early that we shouldn't pay him until we came back. If we paid in advance, as soon as we'd walk away the teenager did, too.

One little fellow who couldn't have been more than 10 years old was going to take us someplace. He wanted 50 cents to be our guide, and he wanted to be paid immediately. Fifty cents was quite a bit of money, particularly for a GI. I gave him 50 cents, and he took off running around a corner of a building. We ran around the corner, too, and he wasn't anywhere to be seen. He was gone! How often he pulled that each day, I don't know. We laughed about it—there was nothing else we could do.

The Mexican shops were great on jewelry, particularly turquoise. But you had to be extremely careful because they would try to pass off as silver something that had no silver anywhere near it. We could also buy some things that were very good. They charged what was to them an exorbitant price but cheap to us.

Most of our experiences in Juarez were very good, including the first squab that I'd ever eaten. It was delicious. I've had it since, but couldn't stand it.

I spent quite a while in El Paso, probably at least three months.

From El Paso, they sent me to Miami, Florida, to await further orders. I knew I'd be going to Instructor School in Midland, Texas, but they didn't have a class starting just then.

The Army had a crazy system, sending me back and forth across the country for no apparent reason. Seems like I could have stayed in El Paso to wait for the school—sure would have been cheaper—but that wasn't how the Army did things.

I stayed in a room with two single beds, sharing it with another transient. I'd be in a room for a short time before being moved to a different room. Others were in the same situation, so every day or so I'd have a different roommate.

One time, my roommate brought out a bottle of Southern Comfort. I had never had Southern Comfort, a sweet drink. He sat on his bed and I sat on mine, talking and passing the bottle back and forth. We didn't use glasses, just drank straight from the bottle. Finally, he said, "I've got to go to the bathroom."

He got up and staggered toward the bathroom. I laughed at him. But when I stood up, I couldn't walk! My legs wouldn't work.

I had no duties while in Miami, just cooled my heels waiting for orders. My training school didn't have an immediate spot for me. That seemed to happen all the time. Even as an enlisted man, whenever they assigned me to a school the school wouldn't have a spot for me until some later date, so the Army would send me to some other location to wait.

I spent six days in Miami and during that time had three different roommates.

I'd rent a car and drive around trying to see some of the sights. I did that twice.

The Army then sent me to Las Vegas. Again, I was in limbo, waiting for my class to start. That was in late 1944. I lived in the barracks at McCarron Field and considered having my family join me, but realized there were no family accommodations available. People were sleeping in cars because they couldn't find a hotel or motel room, nor houses or rooms to rent. We'd go into one of the casinos in the evening and it'd be pretty late when we got back to the barracks. On the way, we'd pass cars parked on the side of the road with people sleeping in them, whole families in some cases. I just couldn't bring my family into something like that.

As badly as quarters were needed, there was no new construction. All efforts were focused on the war, which apparently didn't include building family living space.

I spent about three weeks at Las Vegas before I finally went to Midland. There I trained to become an instructor for bombardiers. That meant back to the tower and the Norden bombsight. That was interesting. After completing my training at Midland —I don't recall how long that took—on the day after graduation I got summoned into the Base Commander's office. He told me that I could go home.

I said, "Really?"

I wasn't the only one who had a conference with the commander about getting out of the service. He talked to quite a few of us, but called us in individually instead of saying, "Hey you guys, go on home!"

He and I talked for a while. He was a major, a career Army man. As a matter of fact, he was encouraging but not insisting that I continue in the service. He was very persuasive, but not in an offensive sort of way. He wasn't aggressive about it at all. I still wasn't tempted to stay in. I had been slated to go to Carlsbad, New Mexico, to teach but went home instead.

They separated me from the service at Great Lakes Naval Training Center (!), just north of Chicago.

I began getting disability payments for my wounds as soon as I got out of the service, and am still drawing compensation. In fact, my disability payments have increased substantially over the years. My disability percentage hasn't changed, but the payments have gone up.

I was in the service for three years, 1942-1945. Being an officer, there was no finite length of service for me, unlike enlisted folks who'd be in for two, three, or four years before their enlistment ended.

I went back to work at Chevrolet in the National Order Department, the same place I'd worked before enlisting. I moved up the corporate ladder, staying with Chevrolet for a total of 18 years. After that, I hopped from one company to another, moving to Texas and then Tennessee. Remarkably, every one of my positions seemed to qualify me perfectly for my next job. I finally retired in 1997.

EPILOGUE

Here are some of my final thoughts, things I want to make clear or things that didn't fit into the main part of this book.

I use the word "guys" a number of times in this narrative. Please forgive me. I should have said "flyers" or "men" or "crewmates," anything other than "guys." I also use the word "beautiful" a number of times, probably too often, but that's exactly how I felt when looking at the things I describe.

There are places in the narrative where I sound pompous, quite a few places where I say "I," and I dislike that. I should have more often used "we" and "they," the latter meaning leadership. In many cases I should have said, "we were sent," rather than "they sent us."

I began to tell you about my early childhood in Massillon, Ohio, which I think was probably nuts and has nothing to do with my war experiences. But for those who are interested, the Erie Canal runs through Massillon and I lived along its banks. Tremont Street is the street on which I was born.

I saw a train pulling coal cars recently. The train seemed to run on forever—don't they always when you're stopped at the crossing?—and it reminded me so much of the marshalling yards at Avignon. Funny how such things awaken old memories.

After we'd been rescued from the Germans, many people questioned why the German officer came to me to offer his surrender, rather than one of my fellow officers. For example, Joe Maywald was our pilot and leader and should have been the natural guy to handle the situation. I'd have to say that it was because I spoke French and could converse more readily with him than could some of my crewmates. I had a rapport built up with some of the Germans. I've got a letter (see Appendix C) in my archives from one of our German guards, and he explains it better than I can.

A few years ago, I located Richard Makoviac's family but he had died by that time. I told them about Richard's gesture, insisting that I wear his jacket when I had been wounded. It made me feel good to give them that little bit of information about him, and they were grateful to hear it.

I tracked down Richard's family through a friend of mine. One day, my friend Jim Beardsley and I were talking about my experiences. I told him I hadn't been able to track down any of my crewmates from the war, and he asked me for their names. Not much later, he gave me a list of addresses and phone numbers for most of them. I'm guessing he used the Internet, at which my skills are limited.

My crewmates were scattered all over the country. I never could find Andy Citara and Ed Weaver, but the rest I did, including Hal Moore's family and Keith Gimson's family. Unfortunately, all my crewmates had died before I reached them. Joe Maywald had passed away just six months before I contacted his wife.

Jim Beardsley died just recently. He was a fine friend and went to Trinity Presbyterian with me. That's in Hendersonville, NC. If you're are in the area and so inclined, you might want to stop at the church and admire all the stained glass in the sanctuary. I'm proud to say that I designed, fabricated, and installed all of that glass and I really enjoyed doing it.

They tore down the old Wade Hampton Hotel in Greenville maybe four or five years ago, around 2007 or 2008. That's a shame because it had been a real landmark; at least it was to me. That's where other married officers and I stayed off-post just before we went overseas.

I wrote to Lieutenant Colonel Perry's family. He led the battalion that liberated us from German custody. I got a nice letter back from his wife. Among other things, she said, "Incidentally, you can drop the LTC title because he made Colonel. Your letter is in his file."

When I got back to the States, at William Beaumont General Hospital in El Paso, Texas, a surgeon named Frackleton took a piece of skin from the inside of my thigh and grafted it onto my finger. As a result, I've got a scar on the inside of my thigh. Originally there had been a spot about the size of my thumb where a piece of flak had hit when our plane got shot down. The flak didn't penetrate deeply but it left a scar. When Frackleton did the repair on my finger, he used that spot on my thigh to get some skin to graft onto my finger. You can still see the spot on my thigh because it has a little different texture than the surrounding skin. It's an area about four or five inches long and two-and-a-half to three inches wide.

My crew and I all entered the service at about the same time. Joe Maywald and I were also about the same ages. Joe was the captain of the crew, a title bestowed on the pilot regardless of rank.

GLOSSARY

.45 automatic, a handgun, semi-automatic actually, that fires one bullet with each pull of the trigger

.50 caliber machinegun, a fully-automatic firearm that fires a half-inch projectile that can weigh in the neighborhood of two ounces and keeps firing them so long as the trigger is pulled

Accra, (ah-KRAH) the capital and largest city of Ghana

Ack-ack, abbreviation for anti-aircraft fire, also called flak

Ajaccio, (ah-JAH-cee-oh) the capital and largest city on the French island of Corsica

Ascension Island, a British Overseas Territory halfway between South America and Africa

AT-6, a single-engine advanced trainer aircraft used during WWII, also called a T-6

AT-11, a twin-engine advanced trainer aircraft used during WWII, also called a Kansan (made in Wichita)

Avignon, (ah-vin-YONE) a small town, now about 12,000 population, in southern France that contained an important Nazi rail hub

B-17, a four-engine heavy American bomber used extensively by Allied forces during WWII, nicknamed the Flying Fortress

B-24, a four-engine heavy American bomber used extensively by Allied forces during WWII, nicknamed the Liberator

B-25, a twin-engine medium American bomber used extensively by Allied forces during WWII, nicknamed the Billy Mitchell after the military aviation pioneer

B-26, a twin engine Allied bomber, called the Marauder and, unfortunately, also called the Widow Maker due to a high rate of crashes during takeoff and landing

Belém, (bay-LAME) a city in northern Brazil located at the mouth of the Amazon River

Boche, (bōsh) derogatory French slang for German soldiers

Bomb bay, the doors in the belly of a bomber aircraft through which bombs are dropped

Bombardier, the aircraft crewman responsible for targeting and releasing bombs

Bombsight, a device used by a bombardier to pinpoint a target for bombing

Colonel Klink, facetious term alluding to the bumbling Stalag 13 commandant on the 1965-1971 TV show *Hogan's Heroes*

Corsica, a French island in the Mediterranean equally close to Italy

Craps table, a shallow, cloth-lined box in which dice are cast during a game of craps

Dakar, the capital and largest city in Senegal, the westernmost city on the African mainland

DC-3, an early, two-engine, propeller-driven commercial passenger plane

Digne, (DEEN-yah), a French commune about 50 inland from the Mediterranean, also called Digne-Les-Baines

E6B, a circular slide rule used in aviation to calculate such things as course of flight, fuel burn rate, wind correction, and time of arrival; still used today, euphemistically "whiz wheel,"

Epaulet, shoulder boards, usually on a military uniform, often including rank insignia on top and fringe on the edges

Euchre, a four-person, trick-taking card game often played for money

Flak, shrapnel from exploding bombs or anti-aircraft fire, also called ack-ack

Franc, a unit of French currency

Geneva Convention, a series of international laws and standards establishing permissible treatment of prisoners and victims of war

Ghisonaccia, (ghee-so-NAH-chah) a small town (probable WWII population under 1000) on the east-central coast of Corsica, facing northern Italy

Gold Coast, an area in western Africa encompassing several countries, so named because of early (circa 1000) gold discovery there

IQ, Intelligence Quotient, a measure of human brain potential or capacity

Lieutenant Colonel, an officer in the Army, Navy, or Marines, an O-5, superior to a major and subordinate to a full Colonel

Luger, a 9mm semi-automatic German pistol

Mandolin, a smaller stringed instrument in the guitar family

Maquis, (mah-KEE) the French underground who were subversive to the Axis forces

Marrakech, also Marrakesh, located in the Andes foothills, the fourth largest city in Morocco

Marseilles, the largest Mediterranean port in France

Me-109, German fighter aircraft, also called a Messerschmitt

Meteorology, the study of weather and atmospheric conditions

Mount Etna, an active volcano on the east coast of Sicily, near Messina and Catania

Mussolini, Benito, Fascist dictator of Italy during most of WWII

Naples, the third largest city in Italy, located on the west coast near the ankle of the boot

Natal, (nah-TALL) a large city, now nearly one million inhabitants, on the eastern-most shore of Brazil

Navigator, a flight officer in charge of plotting the course for an aircraft, taking into account such things as weather and atmospheric conditions

Non-com, an abbreviation for Non-Commissioned Officer, someone of E-5 rank or above, also NCO

Norden bombsight, an ingenious device used by military aviators to accurately deliver bombs, developed by Dutch engineer Carl Norden (see Appendix B for more details)

P-47, a heavily-armed single-engine American fighter aircraft, also called Thunderbolt

PBY, an amphibious twin-engine American plane, also called Catalina or Flying Boat

PX, Post Exchange, a military department store.

Shrapnel, parts of a bomb scattered during its explosion

SS Branch, a notoriously brutal military branch of the Nazi party that grew from three regiments to 38 divisions during WWII, also Waffen-SS

Saint Tropez, (san-tro-PAY) a commune on the southern coast of France, east of Marseille

Tail-gunner, the machine gunner situated at the rear of a bomber

Tunisia, an African country on the Mediterranean Sea

Verona, a large city in north-central Italy

Vesuviano, or San Giuseppe Vesuviano, a commune in the principality of Naples, on the west coast of Italy near the ankle of the boot

VOC, volunteer officer candidate,

Waist-gunner, the machine gunner situated at the middle of a bomber

APPENDIX A
My Combat Diary

Assigned to this group 5/30/44

57Th Wing - 310th Bomb Group
381st Sqdn. Ghisonaccia Station, Corsica

Pilot - ~~W. G. Byrne~~ 5/30/44   Simpkins
Co-Pilot - H. L. Lineberger
B-Nav - E. E. Carman
T.G - E. H. McConaughey
R.G - B. B. Plotkin
A.G - D. W. Sanders

XX under date indicates "No mission"

7/20/44 - Crewed with Gimson and
         Moore
8/8/44 Crewed with Maynard
        and Weaver

⑤

June 2, 1944 -   8 X 500
    Bridges and viaducts at
  * Borgo San-Lorenzo, Italy.
    Targets hit and effectively
    damaged. (3 hrs. 20 min.).
June 4, 1944 - (3 hrs.) 4 X 1000
    Railroad Bridge N.W. of
    Pesaro on the N.E. coast
    of Italy. Target missed.
June 5, 1944 - (2 hrs 25 min)
    Nickeling mission - handed at
    Vesuviana, Italy for briefing.
    Inclimate weather forced
    return to base without dropping
June 6, 1944 - (2 hrs 30 min)
  * Dropped leaflets on Viterbo
    and Terni, Italy. Nine bursts
    of flak from Stimigliano.
June 9, 1944 - (2 hr. 55 min) 4 X 1000
    struck at Pesaro, Italy
    again. Target effectively

June 10, 1944 (2 hrs 05 min) 4 X 1000
Railroad bridges N.W. of
Montenero, Italy. Good pattern
in target area. Lots of flak.

June 14, 1944 (2 hrs. 35 min) 4 X 1000 SAP
Railroad Tunnel East X South
of Prato, Italy. Good concentration of bombs - Light Flak.

June 15, 1944 (3 hrs. 10 min) 4 X 1000 SAP
Bridge and marshalling yards
at Viareggio, Italy. Both approach-
es and yards severely hit. Light Flak

June 16, 1944 - (2 hrs 55 min) 4 X 1000
Bridge (RR) South of Vernio,
Italy. Good concentration. Flak
intense and accurate.

June 17, 1944 (2 hrs 10 min) 8 X 500
XX   Heavy coastal guns at
         Elba. Towering Cu. Forced
         return without dropping.

June 21, 1944 (3 hrs.) 4 X 1000
Viaduct No. Pistoia, Italy. Target

(5)

June 22, 1944 (3hrs. 25min.) 6 X 1000 SAP
Target Vernio (North) Italy. Heavy
accurate flak at Vernio, Florence
and coast. 11 ships lost or damaged.

June 25, 1944 (1 hr 30 min) 6 X 100 Prac.
XX   Practice mission - Bad weather
forced return with load.

June 29, 1944 (2hr 20min) 8 X 500
Railway & Highway Bridge at
Piestra bigure, Italy. Target
well covered. 20 miles from France
NO FLAK

June 30, 1944 (3hr 30min) 6 X 1000 SAP
Rry viaduct So. of Marradi,
Italy. Several direct hits and
near misses. No flak. Col. Ward along.

July 1, 1944 (3 hr 30 min) 24 X 100 -
Fuel dump at Marina D. Ravenna
Very poor results - Bombs hung
up. Light, inaccurate flak.

July 6, 1944 (2hr 40min) 9 X 500
General construction hq. for **Todt**
organization building Florence line. Target
completely destroyed. Poretta Terme, Italy

(6)

July 8, 1944 (3hr 25 min) 4 X 1000
Ry. bridge S.W. Ferrara, Italy.
Bombs fell in Marshalling yards North
of target. Heavy Flak at target & Spezia

July 10, 1944 (3hr. 05 min) 8 X 500
Mars. Yards at Cremona, Italy.
Target destroyed. **No flak.**
Flew with Lt. Brett.

July 11, 1944 (3hr 30 min) 8 X 500
M/y at Alessandria, Italy.
Target completely covered. Munitions
plant also destroyed. No flak. Nearly
1000 freight cars in yards blown up.

July 12, 1944 (3hr. 15 min.) 4 X 1000
Ry bridge at Borgo forte, Italy. Several
direct hits. No flak. Smoke pots used to
conceal target. Bird through nose in pattern

July 13, 1944 (3hrs 05 min) 12 X 100
Pontoon bridge - Po River at San Nicola,
Italy. One direct hit on S. approach.

July 13, 1944 (3 hrs 15 min) 4 X 1000
Rr. bridge Borgo forte - Missed - 8/10
Cu. in target area. 2 missions today.

④

July 14, 1944 (2 hrs 25 min) 8 X 250
Pontoon bridge at Pole Sella, Italy.
Heavy overcast forced return with
load.

July 15, 1944 (3 hrs) 8 X 250
Pontoon bridge at ~~Ferrara~~ Ficarolo,
Italy-Target destroyed- Highway
blocked-Flak once before & 3 times
after target-Mostly inaccurate.

July 15, 1944 (1 hr 45 min) 12 X 100 Prac.
XX   Practice mission- Dropped
12 bombs with fair success.

July 16, 1944 (3 hr. 20 min.) 4 X 1000
Rr. bridge and causway at
Maturna, Italy. Complete de-
struction of target. light Flak.

July 19, 1944- (2 hr. 30 min.) 4 X 1000
XX   Hwy. bridge at Ferrara, Italy
24 hvy guns defending target.
Bad weather forced return
with load-(thank heaven!)

July 20, 1944 (3 hr 15 min) 4 X 1000
Ferrara again- target hit. light
Flak- 26's caught hell-

②

July 23, 1944 - (3hrs) 4X1000 -
    Ferrara again - T/gunner killed
    by flak (P.A. Reed) Heavy accurate
    flak. Target missed. Ironic, isn't it.
    Later reports show hits on bridge

July 24, 1944
    XX   Attended Parker Reed's funeral
    - at Bastia along with Maj. Hill,
    - Lt. Gimson, Lt. Moore and several
    enlisted men.

July 27, 1944 (1 hr 35 min) 4X1000
    XX   Rr bridge at Borgo forte.
    Dropped out and returned be-
    cause of engine trouble.

July 29, 1944 (2hrs 25 min) 4X1000
    XX   Rr. bridge at Ferrara. Target
    weathered in. crossed behind
    lines to Adriatic and up to
    target. Did not get over land.

Aug. 1, 1944 (2 hr 40 min) 4X1000
    Hwy bridge at Balossa, Italy
    Heavy concentration on target.
    No flak!

Aug. 3, 1944 (2 hrs. 35 min) 4 X 1000
France at last! Rn. viaduct
at Breil (N.E.) France. Clouds
covered both primary & alt.
Returned without dropping.

Aug. 4, 1944 (2 hr 30 min) 4 X 1000
Struck at Nice, France
and Sori, Italy - Both targets
closed in by weather.

Aug 8, 1944 (This is "it") 4 X 1000
RR. bridge at Avignon,
France. Attacked by Me 109's
over coast - Flak on bomb
run knocked out left eng.
Hydraulic system & electrical
system also gone. Right
rudder and elevator shot
away. Maywald pulled
beautiful crash landing by
hurdling stone fence in field
Picked up by FFI on the 9th
Surrounded and captured

FFI attacked German convoy
carrying us to Digne. Two hour
rifle, machine-gun & grenade battle.
2 FFI are missing. Reached
Digne after dark and were
"signed in" at Ermitage Hotel.
Attempt to move us to Germany
made on the 15th. FFI road
block stopped convoy. On turning
back to Digne our truck ran over
a 15 foot embankment. Shaken
up but not injured. On the 16th
our own dive bombers hit a
bridge and the town a block
from our new quarters in a
garrison. Plenty of plaster knocked
off our walls. Another attempt to
get us to Germany was made on
the 17th. At the same spot as
on the first try FFI had a road
block. As the 1st truck reached

machine gun fire killing one and
wounding 6 Germans and badly
damaged the truck. Convoy turned
back. Germans scouted for but
did not find attackers. T/Sgt.
Citara became ill during night
and was moved to German hospital
on the 18th. On the 19th while we
were out for our walk we heard
rifle and machine gun fire at
11⁰⁰ AM. This kept up til 2³⁰ PM
when 75's and 105's broke in.
At 5 PM we were moved to a
more solid section of the building.
At 6 30 PM the German captain in
charge of the garrison asked me
to accompany him and speak
with an officer of the attacking
French forces. He asked me to
explain to the officer that he
preferred to surrender to
an American officer. The

Frenchman agreed to the conditions of the surrender and after I had presented my identification tags he agreed that the German officer surrender to me. The German force of 6 officers and 60 men turned their arms, company cash and keys to me. The crew then took the Germans out into the court yard and formed them. At this point FFI Troops gained entry to the premises and only the intervention of the crew saved needless waste of life. The prisoners were turned over to American forces. We were given transportation to Gen. Botter's adv. Hg. and then to 7th Army where I turned over German Co. cash to Lt. Col. L. Perry of G-2.

APPENDIX B
The Norden Bombsight

Today we have smart bombs, laser-guided bombs, and other sophisticated munitions that make missing the intended target almost impossible. But in the days leading up to World War Two, all anyone had was "stupid bombs," weapons that were controlled only by gravity, wind, and other elements once they'd been release from a plane. Before those elements took over, the bombardier relied on Kentucky windage, along with primitive sighting devices. Reliable accuracy required low altitude flying, not practical because of the greater threat to plane and crew from retaliatory fire from the enemy on the ground. Flying at higher altitude, say 10 thousand feet, was much safer for plane and crew, but made bombing accuracy very difficult.

Karl Norden came to the rescue. He was born in Switzerland in 1880. Norden studied to become an engineer and one of his classmates, curiously, was Vladimir Lenin. He immigrated to the United States just before WW-I and went into partnership with Elmer Sperry. Both men were geniuses and temperamental ones at that. Their union soon dissolved and Norden set up his own shop in downtown Manhattan.

Somehow, he became obsessed with solving the problem of how to drop a bomb accurately from an airplane and developed a sophisticated analog computer to do that job. Today, with radar and GPS, that problem isn't so tough but it nettled many bright folks in those days.

Norden got government funding to build his device for the Navy. Meanwhile, his ex-partner, Sperry, had a similarly funded project for the Army. Both were successful but Norden much more so. The Norden bombsight was far superior to the Sperry device. The Army soon switched to the Norden bombsight but had to buy them from the Navy, rather than directly from Norden who refused to deal with the Army. He was temperamental, remember?

Norden claimed he could "drop a bomb into a pickle barrel from 20 thousand feet" using his bombsight. Before then, bombardiers often missed their target by huge distances, sometimes by a mile or more. The Norden bombsight was a quantum leap into the future, and gave the United States a huge advantage over Axis forces in WWII. After spending $1.5 billion to develop the Norden bombsight, more than was spent on the Manhattan Project, the US bought 90 thousand of those treasures.

When not in use, the bombardier locked up the bombsight in a very secure facility. While in transit between the secure facility and the plane, the bombsight would be carried in a box and covered with a canvas cloth. Casual pictures of the device were never allowed. Should a plane carrying one of the bombsights be shot down, one of the crews' most urgent duties was to destroy the bombsight to prevent it from falling into enemy hands.

Actually, the Norden bombsight did fall into enemy hands before America even entered the war. However, the Germans never used the device. Their tactics focused on dive-bombing and releasing their ordnance low to the ground rather than from high-altitude. The Norden bombsight worked great from high altitudes, but not so well close to the ground—not enough time to enter all the parameters.

The Norden bombsight is a mechanical analog computer made up of gyros, motors, gears, mirrors, levers, and a telescope. On later versions of American bombers, such as the B-25s on which Gene Carman served, the Norden bombsight would actually fly the plane through the bomb run while coupled to the airplanes controls. In training, bombardiers could hit a 100 foot circle regularly from an altitude of 21,000 feet (4 miles). In actual combat conditions, accuracy was almost always less than that.

On August 6, 1945, bombardier Major Thomas Ferebee used a Norden bombsight to drop the uranium bomb, Little Boy, from the B-29 Enola Gay, 31 thousand feet above Hiroshima.

Before departing on a mission, the bombardier took the bombsight aboard his plane, installed it, and energized the gyros. Once airborne, the bombardier needed to consider the airspeed of his plane, altitude, temperature of the outside air, any wind, humidity, and several other factors. All these values he entered into the bombsight. Once completed, Norden's invention removed the human element from these calculations.

Gene never flew much over 10 thousand feet and so didn't require supplemental oxygen. Otherwise, up higher in thinner atmosphere, the bombardier crouched in the Plexiglas nose of the plane breathing pure oxygen through a mask. The bombardier peered through the bombsight's telescope and set the target under the crosshair. He had to wear silk gloves to keep his skin from freezing to the metal on the bombsight (another thing Gene didn't have to do), due to temperatures as low as 40 below. As the craft withstood heavy flak and attacks from fighters, the bombardier felt the weight of the mission on his shoulders. Fortunately, once the bombardier had entered all pertinent data, the bombsight did the rest, including releasing the bombs at just the right instant—a bombardier's reactions would have been too slow.

By the war's end, over 45,000 bombardiers had been trained in its operation, each of them swearing under oath to protect its secrecy if need be with their lives.

Oath Taken by WWII Bombardiers

Mindful of the secret trust about to be placed in me by my Commander in Chief, the President of the United States, by whose direction I have been chosen for bombardier training ... and mindful of the fact that I am to become guardian of one of my country's most priceless military assets, the American [Norden] bombsight ... I do here, in the presence of Almighty God, swear by the Bombardier's Code of Honor to keep inviolate the secrecy of any and all confidential information revealed to me, and further to uphold the honor and integrity of the Army Air Forces, if need be, with my life itself.

NOMENCLATURE
AND
OPERATION

14. TACHOMETER ADAPTER
15. RELEASE LEVER
16. CROSSHAIR RHEOSTAT
17. DRIFT SCALE
18. PDI BRUSH AND COIL
19. AUTOPILOT CLUTCH ENGAGING KNOB
20. AUTOPILOT CLUTCH
21. BOMBSIGHT CLUTCH ENGAGING LEVER
22. BOMBSIGHT CLUTCH
23. BOMBSIGHT CONNECTING ROD
24. AUTOPILOT CONNECTING ROD

1. LEVELING KNOBS
2. CAGING KNOB
3. EYEPIECE
4. INDEX WINDOW
5. TRAIL ARM AND TRAIL PLATE
6. EXTENDED VISION KNOB
7. RATE MOTOR SWITCH
8. DISC SPEED GEAR SHIFT
9. RATE AND DISPLACEMENT KNOBS
10. MIRROR DRIVE CLUTCH
11. SEARCH KNOB
12. DISC SPEED DRUM
13. TURN AND DRIFT KNOBS

The bombsight has 2 main parts, sighthead and stabilizer. The sighthead pivots on the stabilizer and is locked to it by the dovetail locking pin. The sighthead is connected to the directional gyro in the stabilizer through the bombsight connecting rod and the bombsight clutch.

U.S. Air Force Fact Sheet

NORDEN M-9 BOMBSIGHT

The Norden bombsight was crucial to the success of the U.S. Army Air Forces' daylight bombing campaign during World War II. Initially developed by Carl Norden for the U.S. Navy, the Army Air Corps acquired its first Norden bombsight in 1932. Highly classified, it gave American forces bombing accuracy unmatched by any other nation at the time.

Initially, production of the Norden bombsight lagged, forcing the rapidly expanding Army Air Forces to use the less accurate Sperry S-1 bombsight. By 1943, however, enough Norden bombsights had become available, and production of the S-1 ended.

The Norden bombsight functioned as a part of a whole system. As the bomber approached its target, the bombardier entered data about wind direction, airspeed and altitude into the bombsight's analog computer, which calculated wind drift and provided the correct aim point. An internal gyroscope provided the stability necessary for using the telescopic sight at high altitudes. When connected to the Sperry C-1 Autopilot, the Norden bombsight provided unprecedented accuracy.

Although newspapers at the time claimed it was so accurate that it could "drop a bomb into a pickle barrel," the Norden bombsight seems archaic by the standards of today's U.S. Air Force. On the famous bombing raid against the ball-bearing factories at Schweinfurt in October 1943, the 8th Air Force sent more than 250 B-17 bombers to destroy the target. The bombardiers used Norden bombsights, but only one of every 10 of their bombs landed within 500 feet of their target. As a result, despite paying the high price of 60 bombers and 600 Airmen, the raid failed to completely destroy the target, and additional bombing raids were needed. By contrast, modern precision guided munitions are accurate to within a few feet, making a single airplane more effective than the hundreds of bombers of WWII.

U.S. Air Force Fact Sheet
SPERRY S-1 BOMBSIGHT
The Sperry S-1 precision bombsight was developed in the 1930s. It was designated as "standard" equipment in March 1941 and was used in some U.S. Army Air Corps bombers early in World War II; however, all contracts for production of the Sperry sight were ordered canceled in late 1943. Use of the better-known Norden M-1 bombsight continued throughout the war.

U.S. Air Force Fact Sheet
HONEYWELL C-1 AUTOPILOT
The Honeywell C-1 Autopilot was an electronic-mechanical system used to lessen pilot fatigue by automatically flying an airplane in straight and level flight. It could also be used to fly the aircraft through gentle maneuvers. When combined with the Norden bombsight, it created the stability necessary to bomb targets accurately from high altitude.

This autopilot essentially consisted of two spinning gyroscopes located in cases attached to the airplane. One gyroscope, called the Flight Gyro, was located near the aircraft's center of gravity and detected changes in roll and pitch. The Directional Gyro, located in the bombsight stabilizer, detected changes in yaw. Using a series of electrical signals, the C-1 Autopilot controlled the aircraft with servos connected to the control surfaces. Either the pilot or the bombardier could control the aircraft.

What the Bombardier Saw

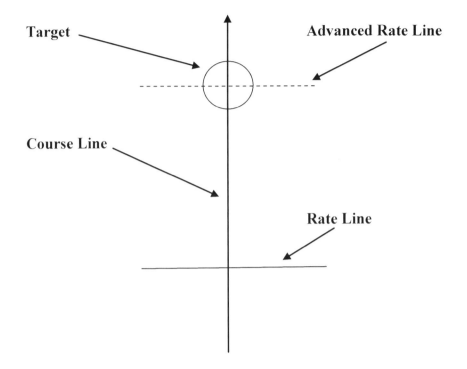

The pilot would fly so that the Course Line (path of the plane) fell directly over the target before turning the controls over to the navigator/bombardier for the final approach to the target. The bombsight automatically adjusted the Rate Line as the speed of the plane changed. The navigator/bombardier would move the Rate Line—we'll now call it the Advanced Rate Line—on the Norden bombsight to create a crosshair over the target. He also tweaked the bombsight controls to compensate for changes in altitude, wind, humidity, and several other factors. The bombsight would remember the plane's actual location, originally shown by the Rate Line. When the plane's actual location matched the Advanced Rate Line, the bombsight automatically released the bombs. BOOM!

APPENDIX C
Post-War Communications

Hans-Eberhard B e r g m a n n,   Oldenburg November 15,1948.
(23) O l d e n b u r g i/Oldb.
Ofenerstrasse 34,
Germany.

Dear Sir,

it is four years now that I had the pleasure to meet you and surely you will be very much astonished to hear from me after so long a time.You once gave me your address and we talked about having news about each other.At first I am very much interested to know how you are now and if you got well through the war.But I must tell you who I am. Well,I am the German cpl.,living just opposite your room where you and four or five other Americans (Cpt.Maywald, one lieutenant and three sergeants of different rank) were living as prisoners in the hotel "Ermitage" in Digne (town of the lower Alpes).Do you remember you brought me back to my room to get my clothings I needed so very much. It was in the evening of the 19 th of August 1944 when you were freed and I became your prisoner.After having gotten my stuff you brought me to the camp with your jeep.I was so thankfull to you,I am still and so often I told my wife about you.Now I want to send you my best greetings and to that of my wife and my little son who is six years of age and a very clever schoolboy.We all wish heartely you are well and hoping this to be so I shall tell you something about my further captivity.

Well in the camp you said very friendly said farewell to me.I can't tell you how much good your friendliness did to me just in those first few hours of being a prisoner. After four days stay in that camp we were brought down to St.Raffael where the Americans made their first landing (near Marseille).When we passed our hotel I attempted to drop a letter directed to you but it was not possible as there was no American in sight.After ten hours journey through the Alpes we arrived at St.Raffael (23.8.44) and started to Oran (Africa) on my wedding-day(26-8-44). We arrived at Oran harbour on 30-8-44,stayed in a big camp till 10-9-44 and joined a big convoy which took us

Letter from a German Guard

to America where we arrived at Norfolk harbour and
at once got a train down to Texas where your friend
Maywald is living.After four days we arrived at El
Paso and that became our camp till our departure
(10-3-46).Well ,I remember you told me about our
future and all hapened that way.There was nothing to
complain of.Treatment and feeding werereally good and
I shall never forget it.But of course the best captivity is nothing against freedom.In May 1945 we were
transferred to an airdrome Alamogordo(New Mexiquo)
where there were big superfortresses.It was a very interesting time.Throughout my whole captivity I worked as
kitchen-police and so I did not get work in the cotton-
fields.I later on did the same work in an American hospital
at Alamogordo and it was a very good time as I know a
pretty good English compared with many others.The only thing
which worried me:I did not get news from my family,so much
the more I was living in the eastern part of Germany.April
1946 I got the first news,my wife and little son were alive.
In March 1946 we embarked in New York.We should go home.
But instead of our arrival in Germany they debarked us in
Liverpool(England).You will understand how much we were
disappointed.From that moment on we were not so very fond
so very fond of America as we had been before.But that is
forgotten now.In England I had to stay till 4-2-47.On
24-2-47 I was so happy to arrive in Germany and meet my
wife for whom I had longed so very much.They had a very bad
time of flight from Koeslin in Further Pomerania(East of Germany). and it looks like a miracle they got through alive.
And live was all they could save.All our property -everything
is lost.We now have to live very simple.Rations are so low
and we often do'nt have the money to buy the food we get by
ration-cards.Some people can buy additional food on the
black-marcket,many others get care-parcels from abroad.But
we are not so happy to belong to these people.Now X-mas will
be in a few weeks.How it will be is another question.Last
year when my wife was working in an English mess our boy got
some X-mas gifts.This year nothing else will take place.
     I am now working in an English Mixed Transport Group and

and this letter is typed in our office after work has been
finished.

I'll close now and hope this letter will find you in good
health. We would be glad to hear from you again. Good cheer
to you at Christmas time and a happy New Year.

Sincerely yours

Kurz-Eckhart Bergmann
and family

Letter from a German Guard (contcluded)

Dear Friends,

7/25/44 —
2234

I've tried my best to come up to your room and talk to all 3 of you, but sometimes one's emotions overrule common sense & I just couldn't bring myself to. I know you understand what I'm trying to bring up!

I realize and deeply appreciate the sympathy you have for me & I also know that when you do see me, you will try to console me, but one has to grope for words under such circumstances, So, consequently, I chose such a time when you wouldn't be here to try to express my feelings.

Letter from Bernie Plotkin
(the crewmate whose wife and son were killed in NY)

From the bottom of my heart I
want to help the three of you get the
interest you're show in the way doing
things what Fate decrees, I've
always thought a lot of you, and now
our friendship means more to me
than ever before; if there is ever
anything I can ever do for any one of you
just name it, & I swear that I'll
do my utmost.

If in the period of the next few
weeks I'm not the same — cos I
appreciate a joke and can't
get around in thoughts, please
overlook it, Bear with me this
period of time, & I promise that

Letter from Bernie Plotkin (continued)

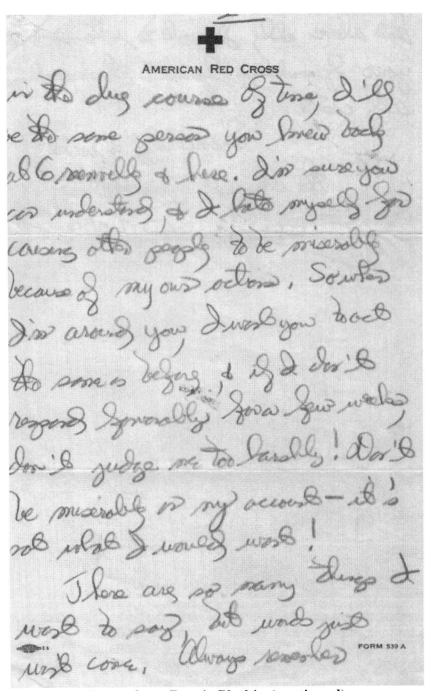

in the drug course of time, I'll
be the same person you knew back
at 6 normally & here. I'm sure you
can understand, & I hate myself for
causing other people to be miserable
because of my own actions. So when
I'm around you I wish you to act
the same as before, & if I don't
respond honorably for a few weeks,
don't judge me too harshly! Don't
be miserable on my account — it's
not what I would want!
There are so many things I
want to say, but words just
won't come. Always remember

Letter from Bernie Plotkin (continued)

178

has above all, I want to retain your friendship forever disregarding all costs,

Sincerely & with the deepest appreciation,

Bernie Plotkin

Letter from Bernie Plotkin (concluded)

Ypsilanti - Mich.,
Nov. 2, 1944.

Dear Lt. Carmen:—

Keith had written us about you and we were indeed glad to get your letter — to know you are home and of course have the nice letter about Keith.

We are sorry not to be able to see you. If you should be in Ypsi at any time would be very glad to have you call. I am at the Ypsi Savings Bank during working hours.

We are expecting Keith home in December. He received his captaincy Sept. 29th. He had planned on 80 missions but said the C.O. said 79 was enough this time and I am glad.

I sincerely hope you have the nicest leave possible and good luck always.

Thanks for writing. Mr. Gimson sends his best regards.

Sincerely,

Mrs. Vern Gimson

Letter from LT Gimson's Wife

180

Dear Lt. Carman,

Thank you so very much for writing to me in October. Your "report" on seeing my husband in S. France was interesting to the thrilling point — for me and to Bill, 16 today and to Virginia at home from college for a week. Every contact means so much and gives us courage as it makes those away

Letter from LTC Perry's Wife

seem a little closer.
Your first paragraphs
kept us spell bound.
The letter goes in Col.
Perry's scrap book tho
he has already been
told about it and of
your good wishes
for further success.
Those wishes were
timely as you see
I'm leaving the Lt.
off the Col. - since
Sept. 24 he tells me.
However, good wishes

Letter from LTC Perry's Wife (continued)

mean complete victory,
home safe and award
or just Lots of Luck
to him and to me.
That's what I wish
you too, as I say,
thanks again for
the good, surprise
letter.
May, God bless us
All and bring peace
and safety to the
world.

Sincerely,
Mrs. L. E. Perry.

November 6, 1944.

Letter from LTC Perry's Wife (concluded)

July 3-45

Dear Gene;

Was happy to hear from you and to know that everything is going O.K. — how does it feel being a civilian by this time? Great I'll bet.

Haven't seen much of the old gang lately as they have just about all left here by now — either on leave or have gone before the boards. "Red", Renkle, the second Lt. a.c. boy, was boarded yesterday and was retired. Sure wish they could get going on me.

My fine to go on my leave now but don't think I'll go for a few days yet as I'm enjoying a "short" stay at El Paso, Oh Boy!

That deal at Dallas didn't amount to much. Just a hand slapping is about all. Of course in writing.

Kathy has been re-assigned here so I guess we won't be loosing her after all. Karl was boarded Friday — haven't heard what he got but he thought it would be six months limited, Simkins got the same.

That you might be interested in the enclosed clipping, the damndest things

Letter from LT Blaes
(a fellow patient in El Paso)

184

happen at that El Ranchotel.

Give Elsie my best reguards and let's hear from you soon —

as ever

Ed

Letter from LT Blaes (concluded)

To Richard Mac Kowiak
4677 S. 50th St
Greenfield, WI 53220

July 15, 2003

Hi, Folks –

It was great to talk with you today and I deeply regret that the contact came after your dad had passed away.

As I mentioned on the phone, he insisted that he give me his jacket after we had been shot down in France. I had been hit with anti-aircraft flak and he was not letting me say, "no", to his offer.

His crew consisted of Joe Maywald, pilot, Ed Weaver, co-pilot, Gene Carman, navigator/bombardier, John Sequenz, tail gunner, Andy Citara, engineer-gunner and your dad.

I was not the regular nav/bom – I had volunteered to fly on this mission.

Like your dad, I have said little over the years about the experiences we had. My family was aware of our tale but few others had heard the story.

The local paper is running a series of stories about the adventures of veterans of any war and someone told them about me – my daughter swears she did not.

The accompanying articles are the result of an interview with Joel Burgess, reporter.

I hope they help fill in any gaps and/or raise questions. If I can help with any information, please do call on me.

Your dad's gesture will stay with me forever.

Sincerely,

Gene Carman
711 Owensby Road
Hendersonville, NC 28792
828 685 2244

Letter from Me to SGT Makoviac

Dear Mr Carmen,

    You found the correct address but Joe died Dec. 7, 2001 - he would have been 84 in Jan. '02.

    I don't know what "channels" gave you our address but I thought perhaps when I sent in the picture of Joe and his crew to "Men of the 57th" magazine and it was printed in the Winter Issue 2002. That some of the crew might see it.

    If my memory is correct you had a daughter Jeanne Dawn? born in 1944. We had a son in 1944 too, another son, who died in Dec. 2000 - and a daughter who has our only grandchild, a boy who starts high school this year.

    When Joe came back from overseas, he was stationed at Pampa (Tex) Air Base as Maintenance officer until his discharge — we moved to Los Angeles where Joe worked at Cal Tech on the Nike project - then back

mailed packet 7/29/03 cc,

First Letter from Joe Maywald's Wife

to Texas where he worked as a pipefitter at Carbide Chem. then at Dow Chem for 28½ yrs. until he retired. That is where he was exposed to asbestos which caused his death —

He stayed in the Reserves until he retired as Lt. Col. — made the meetings and went on active duty once a year —

He loved to hunt and during his working years saved a week of vacation to hunt in the fall & finally had to give it up when his knees got too bad for the walking and climbing he was a founder at the NRA Whettington Center, Raton N.M. and we enjoyed camping and hunting there in the early years —

Joe was active & life member in the Veterans of Foreign Wars, Disabled a. Veterans & Ex Pows — here —

An Experimental Aircraft — EAA was started here. Joe and a friend, whose hobby is building the small airplanes, spent a lot of time at the hangar working on them — We made

First Letter from Joe Maywald's Wife (continued)

the "fly in" (Air show) in Oshkosh, Wis.
several times — a place lovers delight —
the old, new and see — hundreds of
planes, lectures, air shows, etc.

Some small planes & the ultra-lites
are housed at the hanger here — Joe
owned & flew an ultra-lite for a while,
but was getting too old for flight — but
spent time with the planes at the
hanger.

Joe had such strong will power
& kept going beyond the limits of
his illness — I don't know how he did
it — Mesothelioma is a death
sentence — no treatment — no cure.

He was the baby of his family — only
one sister left & she will be 80 you
next month.

This is a long story that covers a
lot of years — if there is any information
that I can give you, let me know.
And thank you for writing — you wish
Joe could have talked to you.

Sincerely,

Markey Maywald

Tele. 979-849-6093

First Letter from Joe Maywald's Wife (concluded)

Ans 9/20/03

Hi,

Thanks so much for sending the paper — all these memories need to be written — after I got your letter I went back & found his "journal" he dictated to me one afternoon years back — he didn't complete all but most is there. My daughter will "Computer it" when she has time & I will send it on —

One question — do you receive the journal or the type of the 57th ? also Ex POWs? If not will send a copy —

Again thank you for writing —

Mickey M.

Enjoyed your letter & the paper —

Second Letter from Joe Maywald's Wife

Greetings!

Hope all is well with you in this beginning new year — the holidays were pleasant here with the children! Our weather is "up & down" as the fronts come through — We had a fortunate year — no hurricanes or bad storms.

I thought you might like the memoirs of a close friend, which came out in our local paper for Veterans day. Bill & Norma were our camping pals until she died of cancer — We went to Oshkosh, Wis. to the big fly-in a couple of times and other places & trips — He & Joe helpful in getting the EAA chapter here. Bill builds small airplanes; he and Joe were co-owners on a couple, Joe spent a lot of time at his garage — When the plane got too big transferred to the hangar. He is helping another guy put one together now. Bill has a sense of humor, they were great traveling companions — He & his wife Betty have an above-ground garden & he dropped off some vegetables last week — Bill quit flying years ago — head condit but stays busy with his hobby —

Third Letter from Joe Maywald's Wife

Hope the new year bring all good
things to you⟶

Marilyn Maywald

Third Letter from Joe Maywald's Wife (concluded)

APPENDIX D
My Medals

JOHN J. DUNCAN, JR.
2nd DISTRICT, TENNESSEE

2400 RAYBURN HOUSE OFFICE BUILDING
WASHINGTON, DC 20515-4202
PHONE: (202) 225-5435
FAX: (202) 225-6440

800 MARKET STREET
SUITE 110
KNOXVILLE, TN 37902
PHONE: (865) 523-3772
FAX: (865) 544-0728

331 E. BROADWAY
MARYVILLE, TN 37804-5782
PHONE: (865) 984-5464
FAX: (865) 984-9979

A.S. McMINN AVENUE
ATHENS, TN 37303-4097
PHONE: (423) 745-4671
FAX: (423) 745-6025

Congress of the United States
House of Representatives
Washington, DC 20515-4202

COMMITTEE:
TRANSPORTATION AND INFRASTRUCTURE
SUBCOMMITTEE
AVIATION—CHAIRMAN
GROUND TRANSPORTATION

RESOURCES
SUBCOMMITTEE
NATIONAL PARKS AND PUBLIC LANDS
FORESTS AND FOREST HEALTH

E-MAIL: www.house.gov/writerep

House Page
HTTP://www.house.gov/duncan/

April 18, 2000

Mr. Erwin E. Carman
1305 Mourfield Road
Knoxville, Tennessee 37922-5912

Dear Mr. Carman:

Attached hereto are the medals you were authorized by the National Personnel Records Center.

I am so very pleased to have the opportunity to forward these to you. In the future, I hope that you will always feel free to contact me should I ever be of service to you.

Sincerely,

JOHN J. DUNCAN, JR.
Member of Congress

JJD:js

Enclosures

NRPM _____ F - I

1. IN REPLY - REFER TO	
Carman, Erwin E. 36 535 887	**AUTHORIZATION FOR ISSUANCE OF AWARDS** For use of this form, see AR 672-5-1; the proponent agency is ODCSPER

2. TO	4. DATE
Commander U.S. Army Support Activity Philadelphia, PA 19101-3460	March 21, 2000

4. CODE NUMBERS FOR AWARDS

1		17	Joint Service Achievement Medal	33	Medal for Humane Action	49	Expert Field Medical Badge
2	Distinguished Service Cross	18	Army Achievement Medal	34	National Defense Service Medal	50	Letter "V" Device
3	Defense Distinguished Service Medal	19	POW Medal	35	Korean Service Medal	51	Bronze Oak Leaf Cluster
4	Distinguished Service Medal	20	Good Conduct Medal	36	Antarctica Service Medal	52	Bronze Service Star
5	Silver Star	21	Presidential Unit Emblem	37	Armed Forces Expeditionary Medal	53	Bronze Arrowhead
6	Defense Superior Service Medal	22	Meritorious Unit Emblem	38	Vietnam Service Medal	54	French Fourragere
7	Legion of Merit	23	Joint Meritorious Unit Emblem	39	Humanitarian Service Medal	55	Belgian Fourragere
8	Distinguished Flying Cross	24	Valorous Unit Emblem	40	Armed Forces Reserve Medal	56	Netherlands Orange Lanyard
9	Soldier's Medal	25	Army Superior Unit Emblem	41	Army Reserve Components Achievement Medal	57	Philippine Defense Ribbon
10	Bronze Star Medal	26	Women's Army Corps Service Medal	42	NCO Professional Development Ribbon	58	Philippine Liberation Ribbon
11	Purple Heart	27	American Defense Service Medal	43	Army Service Ribbon	59	Philippine Independence Ribbon
12	Defense Meritorious Service Medal	28	American Campaign Medal	44	Overseas Service Ribbon	60	United Nations Service Medal
13	Meritorious Service Medal	29	Asiatic-Pacific Campaign Medal	45	Army Reserve Components Overseas Training Ribbon	61	Republic of Vietnam Campaign Ribbon w/Device (1960)
14	Air Medal	30	European-African-Middle Eastern Campaign Medal	46	Combat Infantryman Badge	62	Honorable Service Lapel Button WWII
15	Joint Service Commendation Medal	31	WW II Victory Medal	47	Expert Infantryman Badge	63	
16	Army Commendation Medal	32	Army of Occupation Medal	48	Combat Medical Badge	64	

The Secretary of the Army directs that the following awards be engraved according to current regulations and issued to address shown below. (Engraving to be as indicated in classification or below.)

5. AWARD CODE	6. SERVICE STARS		7. OAK LEAF CLUSTER		8. ARROW HEAD	9. CLASP	10. "V" DEVICE	11. GOLD STAR LAPEL BUTTON		
	BRONZE	SILVER	BRONZE	SILVER				A. ENGRAVE	B. ISSUE	C. TYPE
11									☐ COST	☐ CLUTCH
14	w/ NUMERAL 4								☐ GRATUITOUSLY	☐ PIN
20										
28										
30	2									
31										
62										

——— NOTHING FOLLOWS ———

12. REMARKS Congressional Expedite

The awards and decorations indicated above will be forwarded from the U. S. Army Soldier and Biological Chemical Command, IMMC, Soldier Systems Directorate, 700 Robbins Avenue, P. O. Box 57907, Philadelphia, PA, 19111-7907 within 120 days.

U.S. ARMY SUPPORT ACTIVITY
Philadelphia, PA 19101-3460

OFFICIAL BUSINESS

VIRGINIA A. BARRETT
Chief, Army Reference Branch

NATIONAL PERSONNEL RECORDS CENTER
(Military Personnel Records)
9700 Page Avenue
St. Louis, MO 63132-5100

DA FORM 1577, AUG 90   EDITION OF 1 NOV 76 IS OBSOLETE

1

SPECIAL ADDENDUM
By Jeff Miller

In case you're not familiar, HonorAir is a project where we charter a jet and take WWII veterans, about 100 at a time, to Washington D.C. to see their Memorial. We raise money to cover all costs—it doesn't cost the veterans a dime! Here's what happens on a typical HonorAir Flight:

For this example, our veterans start arriving at Greenville Airport, South Carolina, somewhere between six and seven a.m. Each veteran gets hooked up with his guardian and then goes through screening. In consideration of the physical limitations of some of our veterans, TSA expedites the screening procedure to minimize their inconvenience.

When they get past the security area, the veterans and guardians are divided into red, white, and blue groups. The blue group boards first, followed by white, and then red. We fly to DC. That takes about an hour and 15 minutes from Greenville.

In DC, we begin the deplaning process. After coming up the jet-way into the terminal at Reagan, there'll be anywhere from 200 to 400 people there welcoming the veterans, including musicians from or supplied by the National Symphony Orchestra. Often, there'll be high-ranking officers from the Pentagon in the crowd, too. Everyone cheers and shakes hands with the veterans.

By the time we get downstairs to the buses, it'll be around 10 o'clock. From the time we land it takes about 45 minutes to get everyone onto the buses. We have a police escort all the way to the Memorial. Once we get there, we unload and walk down together—Libby and Bob Dole are often waiting outside the Memorial to greet the veterans, or maybe a Congressman from the group's district or state. They graciously visit and pose for pictures with our heroes.

Once inside the Memorial, we take a group picture. After that, we let everyone just wander around for about an hour and a half. If you're unfamiliar, the WWII Memorial is situated between the Washington Monument and the Lincoln Memorial, just a great location.

We load back onto the bus. Everyone is given a lunch from Arby's and their choice of beverage. While everyone dines, we take a 45-minute ride through Washington with a tour guide pointing out all the significant things to see.

We have a guy from Arby's that we call Ace—I don't even know his real name. I give Earl Morse the credit for finding Ace and he's been bringing our lunches to us, meeting us at the Memorial. That particular Arby's, because of their commitment to serving HonorAir, is now the number one Arby's in the entire country. One year Ace got a BMW as a bonus and another year he got a Mustang. Ace takes great care of us. He packs all our lunches, beverages, and snacks. He's very service oriented.

On one flight, we got to the Memorial and no Ace! The President of Pakistan was visiting and the police had shut DC down for the motorcades moving through town. We needed our lunches.

Ace called me and said, "Jeff, I can't get there. I'm stuck because they've blocked off all the roads."

One of the Park Police confirmed the problem, predicting that the roads would be blocked for at least 30 minutes.

I said, "Let me tell you something. We either need our food and beverages, or you need to order some ambulances. If we have to wait much longer for their lunches, these veterans are going to start dropping like flies."

We had seven motorcycle policemen with us that day. I told their leader that they needed to call some ambulances, or else one of them needed to go get our Arby's truck. They just looked at each other, until I told them I was serious.

"I can tell you right where he is."

They laughed and said, "This has got to be a first!"

Two of them jumped on their motorcycles and took off. It wasn't ten minutes before they came roaring back, lights flashing and sirens blaring, with Ace in his truck behind them. He had the biggest smile you could imagine. That may be the only time an Arby's truck has had a full-fledged police escort through town—the wrong way on Constitution Avenue, yet!

That story is the gospel truth.

If the weather is cooperating, we go to the Vietnam War Veteran's, Korean War Veteran's, and Lincoln Memorials. We spend about an hour there—the three memorials form a triangle. These sites are very easy to visit, fortunately, because we take a lot of veterans in wheelchairs these days. Consequently, the guardians can transport their veterans across some distance, and then let the veterans get out and walk around if they are able.

Normally, from there we'll go to the Iwo Jima (Marine Corps) Memorial. Those who want can get out and take pictures near the famous raising-the-flag statue.

Our next stop is Arlington National Cemetery where we watch the changing of the guard at the Tomb of the Unknown Soldier.

We leave there and go past the Air Force/Air Corps Memorial. The folks there know us by now. So when we pull up, they drop all barriers and let our buses drive right up onto the property. If we have time, we get out and walk around.

All day, wherever we go we have police escorts. We pay each of our officers a fair wage for their valuable service. There are so many HonorAir flights these days that it just isn't right to expect the police to escort us for free. One of the benefits of a police escort is that we never have parking issues.

As we leave the Air Force/Air Corps Memorial, it's normally 4:30 or five, time to head for the airport. Traffic is often heavy—rush hour—but we have no problems, again thanks to our police escort.

We get back to Reagan around five or 5:30, about an hour before we expect the plane to leave. There's usually a swing band there to greet us, with ladies dressed and made up as they would have been in the '40s. The ladies dance the jitterbug to songs like *Boogie Woogie Bugle Boy of Company B*. Some of our friskier veterans jump in and dance, too! The ladies happily pose for pictures with our veterans. All this keeps the veterans entertained until it's time to board the plane. At that point, a gal gives each veteran a big wet one on the cheek, lavishly applying extra lipstick between kisses. What a sendoff!

Once we're all on the plane, we push back from the gate at six or 6:30. Landing about an hour later at Greenville, we come out on the upper level and take an elevator or escalator down. We're all still above the ground floor, but we can see the crowd gathered below. Each veteran is taken down individually and welcomed home by the crowd. The veterans then travel down a long gauntlet of admirers.

It's a long day for the veterans but they get to do just what they want.

We have at least one doctor on each flight, and always some EMTs.

On one of our earlier HonorAir trips, I got off the plane in Washington and set up a boom box so the arriving veterans could hear some patriotic music when they came into the terminal. A nice lady came over and asked me what was going on.

When we told her, she said, "You should have some music for an occasion like this."

"We do have some music," we replied, pointing to the boom box.

"You need something better than that," she declared.

"Can you do better?" we challenged.

"Yes, I think I can," she said, signaling a nearby gentleman to come over. "Jeff, I'd like you to meet Mike. He's with the National Symphony Orchestra."

Every trip thereafter, we've had live, professional musicians meeting our HonorAir flights.

The idea for HonorAir was kind of a combination of things I've read and life experiences I've had, being around my parents. My dad was a WWII veteran; he was in the Navy. Mom was in high school during WWII and her big brother, whom she just loved, was in the Army Air Corps. Harold B. Drake was a B-24 pilot. He got shot down and killed on June 16, 1944. So I grew up in an extremely patriotic home. My entire neighborhood, growing up, was built by WWII veterans, every single house. Every homeowner in my neighborhood was a WWII veteran, except one—he was a WWI veteran.

I grew up watching *Twelve O'clock High, Combat, Midway*, all the war movies and TV programs. After school, we'd come home and play Army in the woods. Everything was about WWII. Veterans have always been my safety net and the people I look up to. That's just the bottom line.

In 2002, my dad developed a serious and aggressive form of cancer. He passed away the last day of that year. My mother lived for three more years before she passed away, too. About six months before my mom passed away in 2005, I read an article in a Charleston paper about a guy in Ohio named Earl Morse. He was a pilot. He and his dad would fly two veterans at a time from Enon, Ohio, to Manassas, Virginia. There they'd rent a van and drive to the WWII Memorial.

Earl was a physician's assistant at a VA hospital and spent a lot of time with WWII veterans. When he found out that most of them didn't think they'd ever get to see their Memorial, he started to take some of them there.

I thought the article about Earl and what he was doing was great. However, I wasn't a pilot and knew I couldn't do what he had been doing. Also, my mom was still very sick, but I filed Earl's story away in the back of my mind.

Six months later, Mom died. As an only child, I had to go through all of my parents' things. In doing that, I found where Mom and Dad were charter members of the WWII Memorial. I was also a charter member of the WWII Memorial, but we had never talked about it. I thought, *That just stinks! Dad died before it was built and Mom was too sick to go see it.*

Dad is registered as a veteran at the Memorial and Mom had registered her brother.

I talked to Tam, my wife, and said, "You know what? We just need to take every veteran in Henderson County to the Memorial who wants to see it. We need to do that in honor of my parents."

"Go for it!" she said. "Let's do it!"

I called up Earl and said, "Earl, I like what you're doing. Have you got any tips for me?"

He said, "Go find a bunch of pilots and start flying."

I said, "I don't want to do it that way, Earl. I want to charter a big jet and take 100 at a time."

"I don't think you'll ever be able to raise the money to do that," he replied.

"Earl, I think I can. Would you want me to name it Honor Flight, the same as your program?"

"No," he said, "This will be tough for you to pull off, but I'll help you with anything I can."

He gave me some tips on who to contact and what to do in Washington to ensure a smooth trip. I agreed not to use the term Honor Flight, but promised to keep him posted on what we were doing.

That was in February, 2006. In March I pulled some friends together, Dave Adams, Frank Schell, Mike Murdock, and David Reeves and explained what I wanted to do. "You probably think I'm crazy."

"No we don't," they replied. "We can do this!"

We went to the *Times-News* and Bill Moss, the editor at the time, did a little story for us. We picked up a little traction that way, receiving about 50 phone calls from interested veterans. I went back to Bill about two weeks later. I didn't make an appointment, just walked into his office and sat down.

"Bill," I said, "how old are you?"

I knew he was about my age, 52 at the time.

"Your dad is a WWII veteran, isn't he?" I asked.

He nodded his head.

"Does he deserve to see the WWII Memorial?" I asked.

When he replied to the affirmative, I told him, "Write a better story, Bill. Make it big—talk to some veterans and quote them. I don't want some little blurb. I want something on the Front Page or on the front of the Local Section."

By golly, he did it! He did a big story that included interviews with veterans. It came out on a Saturday on the front page of the Local Section.

My committee had a meeting scheduled for the following Monday. Mike Murdock, the Henderson County Veterans Service Officer, was our contact guy and his was the number provided in Bill's story for all the veterans to call. When Mike walked into our meeting he was just ghost white.

"Guys," he said, "we're going to need a bigger plane!"

"What do you mean?" we replied.

"Guys," he continued, "I had 98 messages on my phone when I got to the office this morning. The only reason there weren't more is that my voice mailbox was full!"

We knew then that we were onto something. The long and the short of it, we contacted our State Senator and good friend, Tom Apadoca, and he gave us a contact with US Air, a guy named Chuck Allen.

I called Chuck—he didn't know me from Adam—and said, "Chuck, I'd like to charter a jet through US Air. I want something at least as big as a 737, maybe an Airbus. I want to carry anywhere from 143 to 190 people, and I'll need three or four buses once we get to DC."

He asked what I was doing and I told him our plans.

"Oh," he said. "You're a travel agent."

"No, I'm not."

"Well, what business are you in?" he pressed.

I told him, "I'm in the dry-cleaning business."

Dead silence.

Finally he asked, "How much money have you collected so far?"

"None, but don't you worry about that. I'm not asking for a free jet. I don't want you to even *think* that I want a free jet. I'm asking for a *fair price* on a jet. I think that, if you do this right, you're going to get an awful lot of business as a result."

I asked, "How old are you?"

He replied that he was 52.

"Your dad is a WWII veteran, isn't he?"

"Yes," he replied cautiously.

"I'll bet your wife's father is, too."

He admitted that was true as well.

"Do they deserve to see the Memorial?"

Pause.

"I'll call you back."

I knew I had him.

He called me back the next day, saying, "Alright, we can do something."

The numbers of veterans interested in our project had grown by leaps and bounds. I told Chuck, "I want a jet for a Saturday *and* Sunday. You've told me that on those days many of your jets are just sitting on the tarmac, the same for Tuesdays and Wednesdays. Those are the days I want to charter one of your jets. After you've assigned jets for football teams, basketball teams, your junkets to Vegas, and all that stuff, I want what's left. Those planes would otherwise just be sitting there, so I want you to give me a good deal."

I got Chuck hooked up with Dave Adams and they negotiated a per day price in the $30 thousand range. We'd been negotiating with another charter group, who had quoted us a price of $85 thousand; we knew that was a big chunk but we were going to take it until we talked to Chuck. He had given us two flights for much less than the cost for one from the other outfit!

Dave is tough and Chuck's heart was in the right place.

We started building the trip and gathering funds. In 12 weeks we raised around $180 thousand! We've never had money trouble. We originally thought we'd do one trip, then two. When we got back from the second one in September, 2006, the same flight Gene Carman was on, I requested another jet for November. After that, we chartered another one for the following spring.

By then, HonorAir had begun to catch on all over the country. Every time we hit a roadblock, someone giving us a problem, I could find somebody in their organization that had a WWII veteran in their family. I'd just ask them if they thought their relative deserved to see the Memorial. We never got turned down for anything. I didn't try to lowball anyone or get any freebies, just asked them to give me something fair.

Earl Morse, the guy from Ohio, met us on our first flight to the Memorial. He had stopped flying small planes to DC and wanted to start buying blocks of tickets on commercial flights, so he wanted to see how we were doing things. We spent the day together and became good friends.

We buy our lunches from Arby's in DC, the number one Arby's in the entire country. The bus line the network uses actually bought some new buses and put our names all over them because we charter so many buses from them. With US Airways, we're approaching our 300th charters. I was in DC when the 100th HonorAir charter landed and the 200th. I'll go up again for the 300th.

Southwest Air has become a great partner of HonorAir. They gave us something like 2500 seats the first year, and somewhere between 1000 and 1500 the next two years. Free! They've been wonderful. I can't say anything but good stuff about Southwest. They're the official corporate airline of the Honor Flight Network.

US Air didn't give us free seats and I didn't ask or expect them to, but they've kept their prices almost frozen for the six years we've been doing HonorAir. Sometimes it's even less than it was six years ago. They've worked with us in so many ways.

Some of the Hendersonville group have helped organize and flown with many of the initial HonorAir flights from other parts of the country. For the first few years of HonorAir, I spent a lot of time away from home. I spent so much time in the air that my ears got messed up and I had to have titanium tubes inserted. Some have chosen to operate under a title other than HonorAir and that's fine. We'll help them all we can—our objectives are the same. The important thing is to get as many veterans as possible up to see their Memorial and return them safely home.

In February, 2007, Earl Morse convened a conference, the first summit, for people who wanted to organize their own HonorAir flights. At that meeting we shared what we knew. Shortly thereafter, we formalized the Honor Flight Network with Earl as President and developed a business plan. He continued in his VA job for about a year, but then left and went to work for our organization full-time. He became a paid employee, but we really needed someone to hold the reins. It was getting so busy, with groups everywhere wanting to go. We set up a board to handle all that. The rest is history.

If someone from west of the Mississippi wanted to begin an Honor Flight program, we'd arrange for someone from Kansas or other nearby place to coach them and go with them on their first flight. Plus we produced an amazing manual that we send out across the country. We call it *HonorAir for Dummies*. The book provides very detailed guidelines, which Henry Johnson, retired Air Force and Mayor of Laurel Park, wrote with the help of our committee, people from US Air, the airports, and TSA. If someone follows it, the manual should take them through the process step-by-step. We made it as inclusive as possible. We can't thank the folks at Asheville Regional Airport and Reagan-National Airport enough for their help and guidance.

The relationships we've built in Washington are so solid that, if we have a problem, it'll get resolved quickly. For example, we had one gentleman fall at 4 p.m. while we were at the Iwo Jima Memorial. He knocked out two teeth and severed an artery in his gum—I didn't even know there were arteries in gums! I told one of our police officers that we needed an ambulance. We wanted to be sure the veteran got seen as quickly as possible, since our return flight would be leaving in less than three hours. The ambulance came, took a look at the vet, and agreed that he needed to go to the hospital.

I said to one of our officers, "I need you to go to the hospital and make sure the doctor takes care of him quickly. No one is going to stop you from going into the ER, not in a police uniform."

He took off, leaving us with one police officer.

Our buses continued to Arlington. We spent some time there at the Tomb of the Unknown, and then headed back to the airport. By the time we got there, we had about an hour before take-off. We made plans for someone to stay in DC with the injured veteran, just in case, and made contingency arrangements to fly them back the next day.

I called the officer at the hospital and asked, "What's the status in the ER?"

He said the veteran was seeing a doctor.

About 15 minutes before we were scheduled to push back from the gate, the officer called me, but at first all I could hear was a siren. Eventually, I could hear him say, "I've got your guy in the car with me. We're running Code 3 (lights and siren). Have your security people meet me in front of the airport and get him processed through."

Meanwhile, the folks at the hospital had given the veteran a new shirt.

When Mark arrived in front of the airport, TSA folks escorted him straight through security. They came flying down the hall with a wheelchair, the veteran waving and smiling—no teeth, but he was all smiles.

The Honor Flight Network made sure of all his medical bills were taken care of.

That just shows the relationship we have up there. If something like that happens, someone will jump in and solve the problem. Not just at Reagan, but in Baltimore-Washington and Dulles, too. Some HonorAir flights land at BWI or Dulles, and the folks there are just as responsive to our needs as are the folks at Reagan. It's been a good story.

On some of our HonorAir flights, we've passed out complimentary jackets to the veterans. That was when Borg-Warner was one of our corporate sponsors. Otherwise, it varies. We always give everyone commemorative books and videos of the Memorial. We also give each of them caps and pins. The caps help us identify our veterans at sometimes crowded sites.

Nearly every trip, someone will think of something new that we should add. For example, someone with another group observed, "You know, Mail Call was one of the really big deals for these veterans when they were overseas. They lived to get letters from home. We ought to have a Mail Call on all of our flights."

That idea resonated. From then on, during the flight back from Washington, someone will get on the PA system and announce "Mail Call." At that point, the guardians pass out packets of letters to the veterans. The mail could be from, friends, neighbors, relatives, school children, or even complete strangers. A mail packet might contain as many as 10 letters for each veteran. The letters are all different for each veteran.

Rotary groups in North Carolina and throughout the country have added many important improvements to this program. They are responsible for 13 flights just from Western North Carolina. Rotarians have been a huge partner in the success of Honor Flight and HonorAir.

The longer these HonorAir flights go on, the better they get.

The guardians [escorts] are all volunteers who pay their way on these flights. It could cost them $200 to fly from Asheville or Greenville, but maybe as much as $900 to fly from California. You can't buy a day with a group of heroes unless you do it that way. There's always a line of people waiting to be guardians.

The guardians are responsible for meeting with their veterans prior to the day of the flight. We always have a pre-flight meeting where we hook everyone up. If a veteran misses the meeting, the guardian will contact the veteran to tell him what he needs to know.

The guardians always contact their veterans again the day before the flight, reminding them to bring a picture ID and whatever else is needed. The day of the flight the guardians don't tell their veterans what to do, just where to be and when so they don't miss the bus to the next stop. If a veteran needs anything, a beverage for example, the guardian gets it for him. There are always beverages and snacks available on the buses.

The guardian ratio when we first began the HonorAir flights was one guardian per four veterans. It's now often one-to-one because of the frailty of some of our veterans. If a veteran requires a wheelchair, the guardian obviously can't push two wheelchairs. We have extra guardians as a contingency. The Network has put together a group of volunteers in Washington who meet our flights and serve as guardians. That way we have more seats on the plane for veterans.

Because our day in DC is expanded to cover more sites, many veterans like to conserve their energy by riding in a wheelchair until they actually get to a site of interest. For example, the Lincoln/Korea/Vietnam Memorial area is fairly large and kind of hilly. Once at one of these sites, many veterans abandon their wheelchairs until it's time to move to another one. Our buses have lifts that raise and lower our veterans in wheelchairs so they don't have to negotiate the stairs getting on and off.

I get a lot of credit for HonorAir, but it's mostly due to all my good friends. Frank Schell at Globetreks Travel was the guy who designed the day in DC. He went to Washington and walked every step that our veterans would take that first day. We literally knew exactly how many steps the veterans would take to reach each of these sites, such as how many steps it was from where our buses unload to the viewing stand at the Tomb of the Unknown.

We knew that the eyes of the whole country were on us during that first flight. If we were successful, we felt certain the project would take off. If we failed, we failed for a lot of veterans. So we had to have it right.

A guy named Dave Adams, one of my best and most trusted friends, handled the checklist for everything: the money, the numbers, we couldn't have done anything without Dave's help. David Reed is a businessman and an organizer; he really kept us straight. I remember once I failed to get a jet for the first HonorAir flight, but just couldn't get one when I wanted it.

David looked at me and said, "You tried and it hasn't worked out, but I respect your effort. Tomorrow, in our meeting, I want you to sit there and keep your mouth shut. We need to work on a realistic timeline."

I did and he was right. We came up with a very good alternate timeline and set everything up. I lost five veterans, they died between the time we wanted to fly and the time we actually flew. But we did a great job. Had I tried to force it, we may have had an unsuccessful flight and it could have ended the program that day.

We continued to add to the committee after the first two meetings, and it ended up being a powerhouse. I don't know of too many things they could not have handled. They were and still are amazing. Like I say, if I get any credit at all, it belongs to them. They poured their hearts into HonorAir. They're not the ones who got to go meet the President and they didn't get to do a lot of other things I did, but they're every bit as important and I love them for it.

That's the way good things usually happen. It's not the efforts of just one person, but of several. I owe them so much and I never want to forget them. To me, this was a team that worked together as well as the WWII veterans did. It's just that we weren't under fire.

We at HonorAir are very good at what we do. We provide something for members of a generation that everybody loves. All told, we've taken well over 100 thousand veterans to the WWII Memorial, 5000 just out of North Carolina.

There is no controversy about HonorAir. It was such an easy thing. We raised well over a million dollars in this area to fly our veterans to their Memorial. A government entity wanted to give us money but I refused it. I told them I wanted no tax money funding this operation.

I'm always going to be in awe of the WWII veterans for all they did, and am so pleased we could do something for them to say "Thanks." Everything good in our lives is because of them…*Everything!*

Gene Carman, June 28, 2012

18400253R00114

Made in the USA
Charleston, SC
01 April 2013